3:16 PM 41%

RACHEL

THE TEEN GUIDE TO SENSORY ISSUES

Rachel S. Schneider, M.A., MHC

SEND

THE TEEN GUIDE TO SENSORY ISSUES

All marketing and publishing rights guaranteed to and reserved by:

(800) 489-0727

(817) 303-1516

(817) 277-2270 (fax)

E-mail: info@sensoryworld.com

www.sensoryworld.com

ISBN: 9781949177411

DEDICATION

To my camp girls: Sam, Liz, and Abi,
who've changed my life for good and forever.

To my high school bestie, Emily, who made
(and still makes) everything survivable.

And to that stupid marionette.

I am who I am because of you. Thank you.

— Contents —

FOREWORD
by Sarah Norris, MS, OTR/L

If someone had told me they thought I had a sensory processing disorder (SPD) when I was a teenager, I would have laughed. I had long "outgrown" the sensitivity and sensory craving of my childhood, which had been effectively "treated" as emotional or behavioral issues. But when I look back on my teenage years, the hidden signs are all there: I craved deep pressure and alternated between distraction and laser-like focus. I could never find comfortable clothes and had the superpower of almost never feeling hunger, thirst, or pain from sports injuries. I was fascinated by sensations no one else seemed to notice and often socially awkward. I had strange illnesses, pains, and mood swings that plagued me from time to time. But I could wear clothes, eat food, and do all the things I was supposed to. All my quirks could all be explained away by hormones or my insanely tall, skinny frame (I was nearly six feet tall but barely over 100 pounds by age 12—who wouldn't feel awkward or have trouble finding clothes that fit right?)

Rather than feeling concerned about me, the adults in my life thought I was doing brilliantly. In fact, my teenage years were probably my most productive and successful years. I got up before the sun, attended school, work, or extracurricular activities for up to 12 hours a day, and studied nearly every free moment I had. I was a straight-A student, a starter on the girls' basketball team, and involved in almost every extracurricular activity imaginable. I had friends and boyfriends, lots of interests, and dreams for my future. I thrived on all the positive feedback I got. I was doing so well I was even scornfully called "Miss Perfect" by my younger sister. There was plenty of evidence that I was destined to do great things.

My sensory struggles did not become evident until I started college. Away from home, I did not have anyone telling me when to eat (let alone fixing food for me to eat), none of my teachers or classmates knew who I was, and I was no longer involved in sports or extracurriculars. I found it difficult to make friends, got little to no positive feedback for my hard work on my courses, and I had no source for the deep pressure input I craved. I quickly became depressed and anxious, but I had no idea why. I still worked hard, got good grades, and managed to make some friends. I had no idea at that time that some simple sensory strategies could have made a world of difference. I started counseling and eventually got on mood stabilizing medication, both of which did help. I got through college and graduate school, and even got married, long before I began to detect and understand my hidden sensory challenges.

I first learned about SPD in occupational therapy graduate school. One of my professors specialized in sensory integration, and I was immediately enthralled with the subject. At the time, it was still considered a "childhood" condition, and it was something you either outgrew or adapted to by the time you were an adult. We did a brief self-assessment, and I scored in the "definite" or "probable difference" range in more than one area. But because I was a functioning young adult, it did not occur to me that I could still have any real-life impact from those differences.

After graduation, I worked as a pediatric occupational therapist, beginning my training to specialize in sensory integration. I found it effortless to assess and treat children with SPD because I understood their behavior in a way most adults in their lives could not. But despite everything I learned through training and experience, it took over a decade to begin to understand the lifelong impact of SPD on my own life.

It was during my time at the STAR Institute for SPD, as I worked directly with teens and adults, that I started to recognize and understand the subtle but significant ways SPD still showed up in my life. When I left STAR, I dedicated the following year to studying mind-body healing and applying what I learned to myself. Doing so has changed my life.

While my story differs from that of the author of this book, Rachel and I share a lot of similarities. I think that if she and I had become friends as teens, we would have helped each other through the tough times and laughed ourselves silly through many good times. Even though neither of us had a clue about sensory processing back then, we are kindred spirits, and I believe we would have quickly been drawn to each other. I do wish Rachel and I could have known about sensory processing when we were teenagers. Would it have made being a teenager any better or easier for us? Maybe; maybe not. Would it have improved our long-term mental health and physical wellness? Yes, I have no doubt.

So, whether you relate to my story or hers—or neither—I urge you to take the time to give her words some thought. You may just find the key to unlocking some of the mysteries of why you are the way you are—something you may not realize you want to know until you know it for yourself.

— Foreword —

Sarah Norris, MS, OTR/L is an occupational therapist and certified Mind-Body Therapy practitioner. She founded The Sensory Coach, Inc. in 2019 and is dedicated to exploring and collaboratively combining sensory integration and mental health treatment approaches in her work with adults, parents, teens, and other professionals. She co-founded The Sensory Nerds in 2020 with Carrie Einck. Their mission is to support and empower adults with SPD through donation-based programs.

The author, 18 years old
Senior Prom, 2001

INTRODUCTION

Once a Sensory Teen, Always a Sensory Teen

Okay, fine. I'm old.

I'm writing this book for you and I'm not a teenager, not even close. My preschooler is closer in age to you than I am (a thought that freaks me out, by the way), but here's the deal: I would've written this book as a teenager if I could've. But I couldn't. When I was a teenager, I had no idea that I had sensory issues of any kind. I hadn't seen an Occupational Therapist, I didn't have an Individualized Education Plan (IEP); I hadn't even heard of Sensory Processing Disorder (SPD).

The world was just this big, bright, loud, colorful, intense mess of feelings and experiences. At first, I assumed it was the same way for everyone around me. It's like if you were sitting in your dad's car and he hit a huge speed bump while driving fast: the whole thing would lurch into the sky before landing with a thud. Everyone in the car would feel it. They might even look up from their phones for a second. In my case, it felt like the car was constantly lurching and thudding. I figured it was doing so for everyone, but when I searched the faces of other passengers, assuming I'd see a reaction, no one else seemed to notice. When you're the only one feeling the car jolt and shake over and over, you start to feel alone and a little bit unhinged.

And while I usually blame a puppeteer for the official arrival of my SPD (hilarious story to follow), you could say it really started with a single whisper in school. My whole class decided that it would be fun to torture our very pregnant teacher by only speaking in whispers one day. Any question she asked, we replied in our quietest, hissiest possible voices. We even whispered to each other about our whispering, soundlessly laughing in near whispers as her voice got louder, sharper, and angrier in contrast to the sounds of the class she couldn't control.

I was turning 13 and not ready to stand out in any way from the crowd, so I went along with it, even though I was a good kid who secretly liked to learn and honestly felt sorry for the teacher and her big baby belly. Across the room from me, one of my friends hissed louder over the rest of the crowd. Her hushed, once-familiar voice cracked against the agitated bark of our teacher, and in an instant, it felt like something inside of me split apart. My body was hunched slightly in a chair and my arms were propped up on the shared wooden table, but outside of me, the whispers where whizzing by like a swarm of bees. Harsh and prickly, they entered my ears and painfully stabbed at my brain. I quickly went to cover my ears when I noticed how bright the lights were overhead. Squinting, I looked back down at my classmates, but instead of seeing them as solid, whole people, I saw every line and shadow on their faces and every woven thread of their clothes. I felt like I was disconnecting, but from what? I didn't know. I just felt like I was disappearing between the breathy murmurs and muted giggles.

I'm sure I cried. I still felt lost in my skin and in the bright, sharp world as someone—maybe even the poor, taunted teacher—brought me to the principal's office, and it was from there that my dad retrieved me. When we left the school, I felt drained, like someone had taken a needle and slowly removed every drop of blood from my body. He put me in his car and drove me to the pediatrician's office. It was dark by then—I think it was late fall—and I remember the doctor's hallways felt even brighter contrasted with the night. I can't remember how they examined me (how do you check for "whispers stabbed me in the brain," anyhow?) or what they thought was the cause of my episode. The memory ends right there, almost mid-sentence.

That's the thing about teenagehood. This time of your life is about to shape everything else that comes after it: the good and the bad. You just don't always realize when the major moments are happening, so you don't fully pay attention. Sooner than you think, you'll be looking back, reflecting, searching for answers to how you got to where you are. The whisper story is the perfect example.

Honestly, until I sat down to write this book, this memory had been just a little nugget at the very edge of my mind. I don't think I've ever told it to anyone. I never, ever think about it. And then it was like, "Oh yeah." Before my first self-reported sensory shutdown less than a year later, there was this dim sliver of a story that actually meant something. I wish I'd paid better attention. It would be another 14 years until I found out I had SPD.

Some moments you forget as you get older, but the bigger ones become their own legends. It happens in the telling and retelling of stories that felt important at the time and still do. For me, that whisper story was just an early introduction to what would follow. My SPD legend, the first SPD-related story I tell most people—and where I usually say my sensory journey began—is something else entirely.

It was late August 1997. I was a sweet, sensitive, nerdy 14-year-old with soft green eyes hidden behind wire-rimmed glasses and unruly golden-brown hair dyed too bright thanks to the unnecessary amounts of Sun-In I'd sprayed through my strands in the spring. I loved reading and writing romantic poetry, baking my signature chocolate chip cookies (extra bittersweet chocolate and salt), and curling up on the couch to watch sitcoms. My best friend was our turtle, Cookie. I was the sort of person you'd call a homebody.

That summer was an important one. I worked my first job as a counselor-in-training (CIT) at a day camp in what seemed, at the time, like the country. It was where I met a circle of girls with big smiles who made me laugh harder than I'd ever laughed before. There were boys, too, the ones who were eager to spend their hour off each day with us, lying in the sun at the lakeshore or flirting by the picnic tables on a hill. Someone had mistaken me for popular; maybe it was just that I was different, the new girl to an established group of people, and I was shocked to overhear the oldest group of boys, just a year younger, categorizing me as the "hot CIT." I'd also found my first real boyfriend: a skinny boy named Nico with thin strands of sandy brown hair that grazed his cheekbones when he looked down nervously. On that same hill by the picnic tables that summer, he presented me with a silver heart necklace and a letter that I kept by my bedside and read nightly, like scripture.

I was in love with my life that summer. I was in love with my new group of friends, with the boys who wanted to be near us, with the love letters and gifts that signaled my launch into teenagehood. It's something I forget in the telling and retelling of this legend, because what was about to happen was so big and bad that the memory of it overshadows the good. I don't think of the two halves of my story as part of the same period in time, but they were: the best summer and the worst summer wrapped into one.

With camp over, our family vacation was underway. We'd decided to visit Canada. We toured our way through Toronto and Quebec. We walked for miles through a large park. We looked up at the turrets and spires of the Château Frontenac, a massive, historic building. In Old Quebec, we walked along flower-lined cobblestone streets, where I felt almost see-through and floaty. We had pizza at a dimly lit underground restaurant, where I nearly choked on a thick strand of cheese. Wherever we went, I bought postcards and unusual stamps to mail to Nico back home in New York City. It was a time before cell phones. The Internet was brand-new, so the places we went were strange and unfamiliar to us. I didn't see them until I saw them in person for the first time.

My next memory is the center—the core of everything that followed. I always describe it like this: picture a hole in the ground with a long drop down, and land up top on both sides, maybe like the Grand Canyon. In life, we scale so many canyons. We're on one side of the cliff and then something major happens: we lose someone we love, we find something we thought we'd lost, we make a big decision or a big decision is made for us. That *something* flings us across the gulf to the other side. We can't go back to where we came from, because something's already changed forever. We're quite suddenly no longer who we once were.

It was time for dinner in Old Quebec, and the taxi dropped us off at the front of a busy pedestrian mall. A long, metal gate separated us momentarily from the bustle on the other side. It was a summer evening, still bright and warm as we paused for a picture and then turned to walk down the long, busy brick street. My mom was in her bright red vest, my dad in his blue button-down, my sister and I with light jackets tied around our waists.

Our restaurant spilled out into the street, and we chose to sit at a table outside pressed up against the wide windows and ledge. The table was long and narrow without an umbrella or any covering overhead. The waiter snapped a single photo of my family, and in it, I recognize my hunched shoulders and pressed lips as a sign of being uncomfortable. In my legend, I remember this too: feeling as if we were half-inside and half-outside the restaurant, without any barricade separating us from the world around us, steps away from the people moving up and down the block.

After dinner, my parents said they wanted to treat us to souvenirs. We walked farther down the brick pedestrian road, passing all sorts of stores. One of them was particularly bright as we walked in, even as the sun was slowly setting outside, and it was jam-packed with every souvenir you could imagine. Carousels of shirts and pants with the Quebec motto (*Je me souviens*, which translates from French, ironically, as "I remember") splashed across the front nearly touched shelves of snow globes, bells, and stuffed bears sporting the Quebec flag. The music pulsed loudly, as if the manager had forgotten it was a shop filled with stuff and not some dance club. I remember trying to stay focused on finding the perfect t-shirt to take home but struggling because there was just so much going on at once. I caught my reflection in a circular mirror towards the ceiling. It reflected the chaos in the store around me.

I felt a tap on my shoulder, and when I spun around, I was absolutely stunned to be face-to-face with a man and a well-dressed wooden marionette. The man, voicing and moving his little suited puppet, was speaking very fast French in a strange, high-pitched voice, and his tiny friend was gesturing wildly at me. The music continued to throb in the background.

Let me be very clear here. Nothing in life prepares a person for this sort of moment—especially a person whose brain is (unknowingly) not wired to handle and process surprise. This was right up there with the last thing I ever expected to see in a poorly laid-out souvenir shop in Quebec. Or anywhere else, really. You just don't ever turn around and await a French Canadian puppet show for one.

Suddenly, it felt like the entire situation—the packed store, the blinding lights, the music, the unexpected man and his dummy—were sucked into my brain at once. It was almost as if someone had opened a door, and all of this light, movement, color, and strangeness came rushing in. And none of it made sense. It did, logically. I knew where I was, I knew who I was, but at the same time, it was like my brain went "WHAT? NO! WHOA! I CAN'T!" In that moment, I detached from the room and my body. It felt like my eyes and ears weren't my own. It was like I was wearing a person suit and was lost somewhere inside it, but the limbs weren't mine. I saw things in pieces instead of their whole, and they were very bright and sharp—painful to look at. I heard sounds, but not from the outside. It was like I was hearing them echo through the person suit. My body was in this space, and it felt like I had no connection to it, but it was like my brain knew I should and was desperately trying to connect. And this all happened in a second. It was almost instantaneous—the surprise, the pouring in, the shutting out, the feeling stuck, the terror.

I screamed and started to run out of the store. In a strange twist and for reasons forever unknown to me, the puppeteer actually chased after me, shouting even louder in his squeaky puppet voice, shaking his marionette back and forth through the air. I burst through the front door into the warm Quebec night, the blur of the puppeteer somehow still in motion behind me. Meanwhile, I felt like I'd stopped existing. It was as if—what, my body? My sense-of-self?—something was permanently lost. I sat on the stoop, sobbing, thinking: *This is it, I'm going to be stuck in whatever this state of being is for the rest of my life. This is how things are forever, now.* Behind the puppeteer ran my mom, who pushed the man aside when she reached the threshold of the door. She stepped over to me, pressed my face into her stomach, and rocked me. I kept telling her I didn't feel right, I didn't know where I was, and that I was so scared. She kept telling me that it would be okay.

That night, back and safe at our hotel, I described feeling like snakeskin after it's been shed: empty, airborne, flaky, scaly, and without the meat of a body to hold me in place.

To this day, I blame that stupid puppet for everything that has followed.

This story stands on its own: the legend of the girl, the marionette, and the massive sensory shutdown (clearly this book's more amazing alternate title), but if I'm being honest, the next day was equally dramatic and problematic. We didn't know what had happened to me the night before, and so we continued with our trip. It was my sister's birthday. We scaled cannons and castle walls and walked along some unknown waterfront. I look spooky and pale in the pictures, with dark shadows under my eyes, as if I'd seen a ghost. We had dinner indoors that night at a restaurant with a red, blue, and white checkered cloth thrown across the table and wine bottle candleholders. Live traditional folk music with fiddles, spoons, and all sorts of tapping and clacking accompanied our meal. In what's possibly the most uncomfortable photo in my stash, a grinning man with a big accordion looms over my sister's head as I try to use my father as a human shield. And yet, another photo shows me smiling and laughing at the pair of spoons I'm holding as I attempt to add to the haze of sound.

After dinner, we hired a horse-drawn carriage to tour us around the old city, which was lit up in the near darkness. I can't say if it was the scaling of the cannons or the clacking of the spoons or the open-aired buggy in the summer heat, but a few blocks out on our journey, it happened again: the shutting out, the feeling stuck, the terror. Once again, I didn't have the words to explain what I was feeling, so I said the phrase that would become my signal for all of the unknown sensory things not right with me moving forward: "I don't feel good." Scary times clearly call for excellent English. I urged my parents to have the driver bring me back to the restaurant. I remember fleeing the buggy, running, once again feeling lost inside myself. Unable to connect to the sights and sounds around me, I pushed past the hostess, through the tapping and the clapping and the singing, and into the bathroom. I sat down in the stall and stared straight ahead as my ears vibrated. Everything was sharp and bright. I looked down at my hands, but it seemed as if they belonged to someone else.

It's weird to flip through the photos from those three days of that trip. By the next morning, the pictures show a different me: an older, wearier me, the me on the opposite side of the big hole with that long drop down. I look even spookier, somehow—pale and thin, like you could see straight through me. It looks like I'm holding back tears as I clutch family members, desperate to connect my body to anything. And honestly, I was. I usually believe that when a thing happens once, it's random; when it happens twice, it's a coincidence; and when it happens three times, it's a pattern, but it was different this time. Two nights in a row, I'd lost something really important: I lost my sense of safety in my own skin.

Je me souviens.

Even years later, I remember.

❊ ❊ ❊ ❊ ❊ ❊ ❊ ❊ ❊ ❊ ❊ ❊

Right now is bigger than you realize. Every day, just by existing, you're being handed your first templates of everything: this is what true love feels like, here is raw uncertainty, this is the color of heartbreak, here are the qualities of trustworthy friends, this is what makes someone unworthy of your time, here is what family looks like, this is the size of success and the scale of failure. These people, these experiences you're having—they're your personal building blocks. While you're simply living, they're constructing your bones and carrying you into the rest of your life. You're about to be who you are because of them. As each day passes, they're shaping the edges of your personality too: what you like, what you hate, and why. When you look back someday (because you will—time is funny and always moves forward even while you glance longingly backward), you'll realize that the things you experienced and the people you knew linger long after they're gone. They're intertwined with the very foundation of you.

So is your identity as a sensory person. As the events unfolding around you are shaping you into who you're about to be, they're also impacting how you see yourself as someone with sensory differences. With each sensory experience and reaction, you're defining who you are and what it's like to live in your body. You're also teaching people how to treat you and what you need to feel your best. Each time you run into your brother's arms for a deep hug or wrinkle your nose at your friend's new perfume, you're slightly shifting your path forward. What you learn about yourself now—differences, similarities, gifts and all—will impact everything in the future. You could say you're crafting your own legends.

That's why I'm here, as old as I might seem to you. I wanted to write the book that would've changed my life as a teen with undiagnosed SPD, because maybe it'll change yours. I'm screaming back through time at myself, to the scared kid on the bathroom floor in Quebec: *You will survive this! All of it.* Because I did, and so will you. In this book, I'll show you ways to not only survive your teenage years with sensory differences but also live them as happily as you can. Looking back, it's doable; let my stories and years of challenges be your guide.

I was one of you. In so many ways, I'm still one of you. You never really stop being a teenager. You just grow up.

An Important Note Before We Move On ...

Clearly, I was an undiagnosed sensory teen. I wouldn't learn the term "Sensory Processing Disorder" and what that meant for me until I was deep into my 20s. Some of you might be reading this book because you or someone who knows you suspects that you have sensory differences. Some of you may have grown up in occupational therapy, well aware of your SPD. These are two very different paths.

When you live your teenage years with undiagnosed SPD, you don't have the words to describe your challenges or your needs. You might participate in typical social events, go to school, and have romantic relationships, but you feel frustrated by your reactions to some of the unusual things you alone experience. You might struggle to define what's bothering you, making it impossible to explain to anyone. Because you don't have the words to share what's going on but are grown up enough to know that you're different somehow, you might start having negative feelings about yourself. As an undiagnosed sensory teen, I felt ashamed, weird, sensitive, embarrassed, incapable, and broken. I was always wondering what was wrong with me. Only after I learned about SPD at age 27—and worked hard in therapy in the decade that followed—did I start to drop some of those feelings. Nothing's wrong with me; I have a neurological condition. I'd say being undiagnosed as a teen makes many things harder.

When you live your teenage years aware of your SPD, you at least have the tools, techniques, and therapies to live more comfortably. You have the words to say: *I have SPD, and this is what it means for me and what I need from you.* But I do think in some ways it limits you. I didn't know there was a neurological difference I could've worked with and around, and so I was a little wilder about pushing my own boundaries. I think I might've limited myself more to the things I "could" and "could not" do instead of learning the hard way that I'd pushed my abilities too far. Sure, it saves you the pain when you set very comfortable limits on your abilities, but sometimes you miss the chance to extend a little bit further and have a slightly richer life.

So, what's better—the knowing or the not knowing? Who knows? All I can say is there's no one way to be a teen with sensory issues. Neither is better or more challenging than the other; they're just different. Each path requires us to consider different things to make sure we're living as happily and well as we can.

I'm going to do my best throughout this book to present both the diagnosed and undiagnosed sides, but again, my stories are all about my undiagnosed sensory teenagehood, and it's what I know best. I hope that by considering both perspectives, we'll better understand ourselves and each other.

CHAPTER 1

Your Senses and Your Sensory Differences: A Crash Course

All right, kiddies. Buckle up, it's time for school. You can roll your eyes at me (I don't live in the book, so I can't see you), but please don't skip this chapter. You deserve to understand what makes you different and what that means. It's only going to help you with, oh, you know, everything you're doing now and in the future.

Ready? Away we go.

All people live in a sensory world, and we interact with that world (and each other) through our senses.

Pop Quiz: how many senses do we have?

Answer: at least eight, meaning your second-grade teacher was way off. (And your sixth sense isn't being able to see ghosts, in case you're curious. Sorry.)

Most people think we have five senses, and I'm sure you know them, but just in case:

1. Sight
2. Hearing
3. Touch
4. Taste
5. Smell

But we also have these three other important senses:

1. Proprioception (where your body is in space)
2. Vestibular (balance)
3. Interoception (what your internal organs are feeling)

Crazy, right? Why we learn that we have five senses and not more is beyond me. I guess if you're *neurotypical* (someone without sensory differences), maybe the last three don't bother you, so you're less aware of them. But they're real, and they matter, so let's talk about them.

Proprioception – Your Body in Space

Repeat after me: *PRO-pree-oh-SEP-shun*. Say it again. *PRO-pree-oh-SEP-shun*. Look at that, you just won the SATs. That's how tests work, right?

This is the sense of where your body is in space. This sense tells you how your body is positioned. Because of it, you can control your arms and legs without looking at them each time you move. It tells you where you end and the world begins. Or rather, if you're a person with SPD, it might not tell you where you end and the world begins, so you're always smashing into table corners and chair legs, even if you see them with your eyes. Take a peek at your arms and legs. Are they like treasure maps of unfamiliar gashes and bruises you don't remember getting? Mine, too. It could be that you're not wired to know where you are in physical space, so you're working overtime to make that connection, maybe without even knowing it.

Bonus: proprioception calms you down when you are energized, because it's calming to know where your body is located. It gives meaning to your physical being and connects you to the world around you. It also hypes you up when you're feeling tired. Picture getting up, throwing clothes on, and taking a walk. Feeling good yet? Thanks, proprioception.

People take this really important sense for granted, but as we bruised people know, it's one you really notice when it's missing.

Vestibular – Balance

Did you know that your sense of balance lives in your inner ear? Creepy. It's called the vestibular system, and it impacts everything. It helps you stay upright, keeps you from falling when you walk down a flight of stairs, helps you move through the dark, and keeps you alert. If it's not working right, none of your other senses can make up for what's missing. Think about it: if you can't see, you can listen to the sounds around you, feel balanced and locate your body in space, touch objects around you, and use smell and taste to help you understand what you're experiencing. If your vestibular sense goes, you're screwed when it comes to moving safely through space.

If you have vestibular issues, you may crave moving your body and head, seek out rides like rollercoasters, and love being upside-down (basically, you're a bat who likes to have fun). You may avoid these same things entirely—or you may not even be aware they're happening at all.

Interoception – Your Internal Sense

Hungry? Cold? Sleepy? Racing heart? Have to pee? You know how your body is feeling thanks to your eighth and final sense, interoception. It's basically the inside of your body's voice. If your stomach, heart, and other organs could speak to you, what would they say? *FEED ME. PUT ON A COAT. SLOW DOWN. FIND A BATHROOM.* The body's main goal is to stay balanced. The problem for people with SPD is that we don't always hear what our organs are saying. Or we hear them too loudly. Or we don't like what we hear. If you never remember to eat, that could be interoception. If you run to the bathroom every 20 minutes, that could be interoception—or a urinary tract infection. Quick, go see a doctor just in case.

When I was in college, I wanted to volunteer with a local afterschool program. I lived just off of my suburban campus with no car, so the director of the program offered to drive five minutes out of her way to pick me up and bring me to my first day of training. I stood waiting for her by the train station, a few steps away from my quad, as we'd agreed. It was late fall in Boston (so it was pretty much the Arctic outside), and wanting to look professional for my first day, I wore a fancy fall coat, my favorite boots, and a light pair of new gloves. I'd purposefully forgotten my new hat. I hated hats. The Massachusetts wind thought I was hilarious in my thin little outfit and blew and blew at me as I waited for my ride.

Still outside a full hour later with no car in sight, I thought: *Call Mom.* Not sure why. My mom was in New York City, but I realized that I was having trouble thinking. When she picked up, I started to cry and slur my words. It felt thick to speak, like I'd shoved a spoonful of honey into my mouth before making the call. She asked me if I was feeling cold. Who, me? Nope. I never, ever felt cold, and besides, I was in a coat. The more we spoke, the more she realized I checked the boxes for hypothermia. Yes, you heard me, hypothermia, like the thing that happens to lost hikers stranded on a mountaintop in an Oscar-winning movie. Except I was a college student waiting for a ride to her internship down the street from her dorm just outside of Boston. At that moment, the director drove up, and I piled my frozen body into her car, my tears clinging like frost to the sides of my cheeks. She'd forgotten to pick me up, and I had become so cold so quickly that it never occurred to me to call her or go inside. The scariest part? My body never registered that I was cold. I would've waited out there for an eternity, Rachel the Human Popsicle. She blasted the heat as she drove me around the corner to my dorm. I never saw her again.

Years later, I know that interoception played a leading role in this legend. While I feel my heart racing more than most and the need to eat and use the bathroom, I rarely notice cold temperatures, so most days, I live like a poorly informed polar bear in my kingdom of ice. Even growing up, after we turned out the light at night, I always fiddled with the knob on the air conditioner in the room I shared with my sister. My parents would wake us up in the morning, their wintry breaths visible in the dim light, saying that it felt cold enough to hang meat in there. I'd emerge from my chilly coma like I'd been happily hibernating.

People without sensory issues barely think about this sense. It's automatic. Hungry? Eat. Need to go to the bathroom? Go. Heart racing? Stop. Typically wired people deal with interoception without having full, meaningful conversations with it.

The Moral

These last three senses become obvious when they're not working well. It's no surprise, because they're things we feel inside that are impossible to see. But that's the problem. If we've always felt this way, it's hard to know that what we're feeling is not what everyone else around us feels. It's like the analogy I used earlier of sitting in a car that keeps bumping up and down on the road, but you're the only person who seems to notice.

We all just assume that how we experience the world is similar to everyone else. That's not always the case, and sometimes we live clueless and uncomfortable.

RACHEL

All right, class, what have we learned so far?

1. We live in a sensory world.
2. We have eight senses, not five.
3. Sometimes our senses don't work the way they do for most people.

That last one is important—it's actually the reason I'm writing this book, but I suspect you already know that. For some of us, our senses aren't making sense of the information they're given. Maybe our eyes see, but what we see feels overwhelming, sharp, and bright. Or our ears hear, but the sounds aren't as loud or intense as we like. Maybe we can't figure out if we're hungry or have to pee, and so we rarely do either.

Ask yourself these questions:

- ☑ Do your senses bother you?
- ☑ Do you have sensitivities that get in the way of living your life the way you want?
- ☑ Do you feel like you struggle to do basic human stuff because of your senses?

If so, you might have sensory issues. And I'm sure if you're a teen reading this book, you either know you have sensory issues (yay!) or you're wondering if you do—or maybe even someone you love is wondering if you do. (It's also a yay, by the way.)

Sensory Issues

So, what are "sensory issues"? What I mean is this: your senses might be working in a typical way. For example, you can hear and see without any problems. You're not blind or deaf. But the way your brain makes sense of what you're hearing, seeing, tasting, touching, and experiencing through the eight senses is different. Your reaction is also different. Whereas someone without sensory issues might be able to ignore the roar of a fire engine as it speeds by, you might feel scared or overwhelmed by the noise. Or maybe you can't get enough of a particular smell, so you look for it wherever you go, to the point of feeling uncomfortable without it. Maybe you can't find something in your backpack with your hands without looking. It's unusual, because most people don't struggle with the same things. (Sorry, boo.)

Types of Sensory Issues

There are a few kinds of SPD. You may have one; you may have more. They can feel a little bit complicated, but I believe in you and the power of reading stuff. So, onward!

Sensory Modulation Disorder

You may have trouble controlling the amount of sensory input your brain takes in, so you crave, avoid, or ignore sensory information. This is called Sensory Modulation Disorder and is one of the most common types of SPD.

1. **You CRAVE.** "Crave" means "to want something so badly that you look everywhere to find it." I'm sure you've craved a bag of potato chips or a sandwich before. Now picture craving a hug—needing one so badly that you don't feel right until you get one. By craving a hug, you're actually looking for deep touch and proprioceptive input from someone outside of your body. If you're craving the smell of baking cookies and feel miserable until you smell it, you're actually looking to interact with your sense of smell because it makes you feel good. Also, cookies smell delicious, so I'm with you.

2. **You AVOID.** "Avoid" means "to stay away from something or someone no matter what." Maybe you avoid cleaning the dishes because you think it's boring. Or you avoid the loud guy in your class because he teases you. Now picture avoiding flashing lights because they make you feel uncomfortable. Imagine avoiding high fives and fist bumps because they make your skin feel funny. By shying away from these, you're actually saying your body often doesn't like sight or touch.

3. **You IGNORE.** "Ignore" means "to not pay attention to something or someone." Maybe you ignore your little brother when he whines about having to nap or you ignore your phone when you're not in the mood to talk to someone. Imagine not even noticing that you got ketchup all over your hands, so you end up wiping it everywhere. Picture someone calling your name over and over, but you somehow don't realize it. You're not noticing touch or sound, because you're ignoring these sorts of sensory input.

Most sensory people interact with their senses in some combination of craving, avoiding, and ignoring. You may love touch but hate sounds, especially when they're unexpected, and like me, you might have zero clue where your body is in the space around you, so you walk into everything. Funsies.

Sensory Discrimination Disorder

Some people can't understand the qualities of a sense, such as their location, feel, or weight. If you hear a siren and turn your head the wrong way to look at it, reach into a dark drawer and can't figure out what you're feeling, or hold something too hard or too softly in your hands (and you smush it or drop it), you may have issues with sensory discrimination.

Sensory-Based Motor Disorder

Stuck in a body that doesn't do what your brain asks? It could be that you have a Sensory-Based Motor Disorder. Someone with this has trouble standing without slouching, sitting up straight, or planning their movements to do something, like catching a ball in a glove. If you have this, you might always feel clumsy and uncoordinated.

So ... Who Has Sensory Issues?

Lots of people, actually. People on the Autism Spectrum, people with Attention Deficit Hyperactivity Disorder (ADHD), people with Post-Traumatic Stress Disorder (PTSD), and also people with SPD, like me. Because I have SPD, and it's what I know best, let's take a quick trip to science class so I can really explain it to you.

The Science Part

I warned you and I'll warn you again: this is the science part of the book. If you're big into science, hooray for you, this should be exciting! If you're not, that's okay too. If you have SPD and want to know why and what it looks like inside your head, keep reading. It's pretty amazing stuff, and I'll try to make it as simple as I can.

SPD is *neurological*. That means it relates to the structure of the brain—the actual, physical, squishy-looking brain in your skull. It's not *psychological*, which relates to the ways we think and act and is sometimes impacted by chemicals in the brain.

Something is physically different in the brains of people with SPD. Three researchers at UCSF Benioff Children's Hospital in San Francisco proved this in 2013. To understand what's different, you need to know that there are two types of tissue in the brain: white matter and grey matter. The white matter is like a subway or a train. Its job is to connect the grey matter, which are the parts of the brain that do the processing of things like sensory information. In people with SPD, the white matter is less well-connected in areas where it should be better connected. This means that people with SPD have brains that act differently when it comes to processing input from the eight senses. Sensing, especially from more than one sense at once, and making sense of the information does not happen quickly or well. This makes the processing of sensory information especially tough—and sometimes impossible—purely because of how our brains are built. The study in 2013 was huge, because it proved that SPD exists and can be seen.

Another study by the same team a few years later compared brains of children with SPD to brains of children with Autism Spectrum Disorder (ASD). It turns out that there's more disconnection in the sensory areas of white matter in SPD brains than in ASD brains. This means that while people with ASD also have sensory sensitivities, it's more intense for people with SPD. They also found that ASD brains show a difference in the area of the brain responsible for processing facial emotions (like expressions) and language, but much less so for people with SPD. This means that people with SPD don't typically struggle with these things. This study was a big deal, because it proved SPD and ASD aren't the same thing, meaning SPD is its own neuro-logical difference.

Whew.

Did I lose you? I feel like I lost myself there between the matter and the colors and the areas. The brain is complicated, and describing it to anyone is extra complicated. If that felt overwhelming, I can break it down here even further and just say this:

Our SPD brains are built differently. Science proves it.

And that really matters to me as someone with SPD who went undiagnosed for 27 years. It means I'm not making it up when it feels like my brain is being attacked by the act of looking. It makes room for the moments my brain shuts down, like it did in that souvenir shop in Canada. It proves it's not something else by itself, like a psychological disorder. It gives me permission to finally be me—and maybe, even, for you to finally be you.

Some Terms Before We Move On

Because I don't know where else to put these super-important sensory words, I'm putting them here. You'll need them to understand yourself and your experiences as we move through this book, so read up, kid:

- *Dysregulation* is when you can't regulate yourself (calm down or energize) to be neutral. It's like being on a see-saw in a playground; you're either very up or very down, almost buzzing with energy or so sleepy and sluggish that you don't want to do anything.

- When you're *regulated,* you're in a nice, calm, neutral place within yourself and ready to act on whatever comes next. It's important to be regulated and know how to self-regulate so you can live your happiest life. Treatment, tools, and techniques help this, so see Chapter 12 for tips.

- *Sensory meltdowns* might look a little bit like a childhood tantrum. You feel emotionally dark and stormy. You might scream and yell or even cry big sobs. When you become alert again afterwards, it almost feels a little bit like waking up, and you may feel emotionally drained and sleepy. Quiet, dark, calm spaces are the best places to ride out a sensory meltdown. It's always temporary.

- *Sensory shutdowns* are usually confused with senso-ry meltdowns, but I promise you they're different. In a shutdown, your brain seems to give up making sense of sensory information. Sounds, sights, smells, tastes—all senses might feel warped and weird. You may feel like your brain is taking a tiny step back from a bunch of overwhelming things, or (as is more common for me), you might feel like you're entirely disconnected from your body and the world around you. Quiet, dark, calm spaces are the best places to ride out a sensory shutdown, too. It can feel scary, but it's also always temporary.

- Meltdowns and shutdowns usually happen in the face of *sensory overload*, which is when your brain has too much information from too many different senses to process at the same time. You may feel overwhelmed. If you're able to get to a quiet, dark, calm space before it gets too bad, you might be able to avoid the meltdown or shutdown entirely.

CHAPTER 2
The Shift

One day, you're a kid playing video games and collecting stickers (or whatever kids do these days—I'm old, remember?) and then suddenly you have hair in weird places and are greasy, cranky, and super emotional. (It's cool, you're gross; same goes for literally every person who ever hit puberty, BTW). Now imagine you're you—maybe a normally extra-aware, super-sensitive person—making the same shift. Even if you were handling your undiagnosed sensory childhood and tweenagehood like a champ, something changes when you make that transition from childhood to adolescence.

Maybe you were diagnosed as a kid: a skilled wearer of noise-cancelling headphones and user of weighted blankets, usually able to manage whatever sensory garbage was thrown your way. Or maybe you were undiagnosed: quick to cry, quick to overwhelm, but mostly functional within reason. It doesn't matter either way, because one thing changes for all of us.

Hormones.

Screw you, hormones! *Shakes fist*

Or rather, thanks, hormones ... I guess? You wouldn't be able to grow up without them. But they're the reason that whatever your situation in childhood, you're probably feeling your sensory sensitivities more now. It's a theory that leading SPD researchers have about our challenges in adolescence, although no studies have focused on this just yet. But, it makes sense. Hormones surge, and you go from a pretty-faced person to a pimple wrangler. There's hair and sweat and fluids and just other icky stuff you've never dealt with before. If you're sensitive to touch, the feel of these things on your body might make your skin crawl. On top of that, *interoception*, that sense of what your inner organs are feeling, is thrown totally out of whack. Plus, you're growing, which makes knowing where your physical body is in space (aka *proprioception*) extra challenging. That's the sense that keeps you feeling calm and regulated, but it's hard to *keep calm and sensory on* when you're in the middle of a growth spurt.

Now, let's heap on top of this hormone BS the fact that your life is changing—your sense of self, goals, responsibilities, social and educational requirements, family lives, romantic lives, and your place within your culture and maybe your religion are all shifting. Sorry; take a deep breath. I felt the stress of that sentence writing it, and I'm 38. Because really, it's a big time in your life. If you read the intro like a good reader, you know I get it especially. It's a big deal to be a teenager. Everything across all areas of your life is changing to help you finish growing into Adult You. Take biology's hormonal tricks, mix in some real-life chaos, and of course you're feeling your sensory differences more now.

In case you're curious, we're challenged throughout our lives to deal and re-deal with our sensory sensitivities. If you were diagnosed in childhood, I'm sure you did some excellent rewiring through occupational therapy (OT). If you weren't diagnosed, that's cool, too; your brain is still growing, so going through OT now will still make a difference in your life. But you know—and I know—SPD doesn't just go away. It changes as we change and face new challenges. And life is nothing if not ever-changing and filled with challenges.

So, think of this shift as the first big one in your life. Your sensory differences are being put to a significant test. If you notice them flaring up or just showing up and taking center stage for the first time, know you're not alone.

CHAPTER 3
The Fun You: Social Life

For a split second at the start of high school, I was almost popular. Almost. It was quick enough that if you blinked, you might've missed it. But I saw it. The problem was the timing. The summer before ninth grade was the summer of camp and the marionette, and days before high school started, I stood at the door of my mom's home office, crying. Something was wrong with me. I was scared all the time—even more so since the unexplainable episodes in Canada. I needed to see a therapist. My mom knew it. I knew it. I suspect even the marionette knew it deep down in his cold, wooden heart.

The psychologist's name was Lisa, and she met me at her office with corkscrew curls and a thin smile. It was awkward sitting on a living room couch and talking to this stranger about the series of events in Quebec that had triggered our meeting.

I remember her asking me questions about the episodes: *Does your heart race? Do you feel like you could die? Do you think you're having a heart attack?* I didn't know—I was 14, what did I know about heart attacks?—so I said maybe. Her diagnosis was quick: Panic Disorder, a psychological disorder where a person fears having intense episodes of anxiety called *panic attacks*. She was the grown-up and the professional, and I was, well, one of you, so I said, *Okay, that must be it.* I should've explained the situation better. I should've mentioned the bright lights and loud club music and the surprise of the puppeteer. I should've talked about the clacking spoons and the fiddles and accordion. But I didn't know the right words to use to say "When I lose temporary touch with my immediate world, it's my senses that suffer, and it's scary."

When I started high school, I was in therapy for an anxiety disorder. But I was still me—friendly, engaging, always nerdy, as you already know—and people wanted to be my friend. A new girl, Liza, immediately decided we were best friends. She scribbled our names in her notebook with hearts and "BFF," and because she was clearly so much more outgoing and social than I was, I let her, even if I wasn't sure about the whole thing. Boys adored her southern charm and auburn hair, and she was invited to the full span of high school parties and gatherings. I was invited too, because we were a package deal—at least on paper. But while Liza would show up to bowl late Sunday night or sneak cigarettes and beer down by the marina, I would always make up excuses about why I couldn't make it. How could I tell her and the popular ninth graders that I was afraid of having what I was told were panic attacks in public? I wasn't going to get a fake ID and take the subway downtown after dark to sneak into our grade's favorite live music club, because the truth was I could barely make the two-block walk home from the city bus comfortably alone during the daytime.

Late that fall, the social invites stopped coming. By the winter, Liza and I were friendly at a distance. I still sat patiently in the stairwell and gave her advice during her bouts of boy-friend troubles. She still brought me flowers on my birthday, armfuls of which were the true measure of popularity for my grade. But I wasn't popular, not at all.

I didn't mind too much, because I had my new group of camp friends. It was pictures of their faces that I taped up in my locker. That time we had a food fight with cupcakes on Alyse's birthday. That other time Louise and Jaclyn and I had our hair French-braided. Pictures of our sleepovers and stretching out in our bathing suits and watching the annual canoe race. At night, I had hour-long calls with Beth, who'd tell me every little detail about her day: how everyone was, the latest gossip. I had dates with Nico. Although I didn't live near them, I adored them, I was a part of them, and I knew I had them, so I didn't care as much as I otherwise might have about who did or didn't like me at school.

Except one person. Let's call her Mandy. Mandy was nasty and insecure. Known for being the daughter of an alcoholic father and obsessively strict mother, she wasn't so much popular in my grade as she was feared by everyone in my grade. She wasn't particularly clever; she was mean, and she looked plain. People were nice to her purely to stay on her good side. She thought that meant she had lots of friends, and it gave her permission to be cruel in whatever way she saw fit. Namely, making my life miserable. It's possible it was because everyone knew I came from a happy home, or maybe it was because I was always so damn nice, but she despised me. I honestly have no idea what I did to piss her off or why she felt the need to carry on hating me from middle school into high school, but carry on she did. For all the upset she caused, years later I (thankfully) can't remember the specifics, but I do remember crying about her one afternoon in my bedroom. Looking out at the tall buildings of New York City, I spoke to myself as an adult in the future. I said I couldn't wait to grow up so I would never have to deal with Mandy again. I'm happy to report that I haven't seen or heard from her in nearly 20 years.

* * * * * * * * * * * *

In the fall of 10th grade, I lost my camp friends. In a turn of events that makes us laugh now so many years later, Jaclyn gave me permission to date her ex-boyfriend, James. But she wasn't really okay with it and I wasn't willing to let him go, so everyone stopped talking to me. Taking down their photos from my locker, I felt sad and alone. They'd become such a part of my identity over the past two summers, and it hurt to suddenly be left without their calls, sleepovers, and inside jokes. I put up pictures of me and James instead.

A few weeks later, I tried out for my school's Junior Varsity volleyball team. I've never been particularly coordinated or interested in sports, but I loved the idea of belonging to something. Of succeeding. At the first tryout, I was practicing my underhand serve when a girl came to practice beside me. I'd been at the school since kindergarten and I'd never seen her before, so

I made a funny comment about how just okay I was at volley-ball. She laughed and made a similar comment back. Her name was Charlotte, and it sounds crazy, but she felt familiar, like we'd always known each other. Like we operated on the same energy level. She was, indeed, new; she'd been at our school's counterpart for years, and she was in the grade below me. We both made the team and instantly became friends. When we had away games, we sat together in the van and talked trash about the schools and teams we were about to beat. Charlotte was like me: studious, serious, nervous, silly, and quite possibly the brightest, warmest, most wonderful human being to grace the planet. When her grandmother passed away, Charlotte came to school wearing her worn button-down shirts and antique necklaces, softly crying into the freshly baked cafeteria chocolate chip cookies I pressed into her hands. Together, we got involved in the school play that year: *Grease*, the popular 1950s greaser high school romance musical. Charlotte worked on the costumes while I acted.

✶ ✶ ✶ ✶ ✶ ✶ ✶ ✶ ✶ ✶ ✶

A side-note about *Grease*. Know what's scary? Being an undiagnosed teen with sensory issues and anxiety and trying out for the school musical. No, scratch that. Being an undiagnosed teen with sensory issues and anxiety and *actually getting cast* in the school musical. But, once again, I wanted to belong to something. To succeed. To prove I was just like everyone else. When I first tried out for the play, I auditioned for Patty Simcox, the peppy, beautiful, and brilliant cheerleader who had just enough lines to be dangerous. Of all the characters, popular Pink ladies included, I wanted to be the smart and perky one. Instead, I was offered the role of the tightly wound teacher, Mrs. Lynch (yes, I know, not much of a character stretch for me). The catch: I had the first few lines of the entire musical. The whole production hinged on my walking out onto an empty stage alone at night in front of a full theater and delivering my lines under a bright spotlight.

The night of our first of three performances, as the lighting crew dimmed the stage lights and the hallway outside the theater buzzed with our audience, I was on the other side of the auditorium doors with the director. I was so anxious that my jaw had clamped itself shut and I couldn't open my mouth. The director's wife came over to rub my face and help me focus on some deep breathing. And then the audience filed in, and I walked out and delivered my lines perfectly. Terrifying—yes, especially towards the end of the musical, when I had to sit on the side of the stage and watch the dance contest. Pairs of classmates whirled around me to the quick beat of "The Hand Jive," a classic *Grease* song. Between the bright lights, movement, and sound, I clung to the pointed edge of the stage and forced myself to stay focused and not give in to the feeling of overwhelm that crept across my skin.

My impersonation of a strict 1950s teacher was met with excellent reviews. I managed to survive the intense anxiety and unidentified sensory sensitivities. I might've even had some moments of fun, and I haven't acted since.

❉ ❉ ❉ ❉ ❉ ❉ ❉ ❉ ❉ ❉ ❉ ❉

Once Charlotte and I became close friends—you might even say high school besties—a small social circle built around us. We were the unpopulars, the smart and quirky people who sat at the tables along the edge of the cafeteria instead of in the middle. Joining us were a best friend duo and co-editors of the yearbook named Katherine and Ann (more commonly known as *KathandAnn* because you never saw or spoke to one without the other), and Tom, my Australian best guy pal. There might have been others who floated in and out, but it was this little non-group group that saw me safely through the end of high school.

Decades later, Charlotte and I still talk at least once a week. Instead of volleyball and rival teams, it's about our daughters, our partners, and our families. It's been long enough to believe that we really have always known each other. And she's still quite possibly the brightest, warmest, most wonderful human being to grace the planet.

The Great Friend Conundrum

Let me guess: you really want friends, but you can't handle the social events that come with them. Or you really want friends, but you're afraid to tell them about your sensory issues, so you keep people at a distance. Maybe you have a huge group of lifelong friends who understand and celebrate your differences (lucky you!) Maybe you're tired of being alone. Maybe you crave being alone but feel lonely. Social lives are complicated in general. For those of us with SPD, our social lives directly relate to our sensory needs. When we consider making friends at any age, we ask ourselves some of the following questions:

1. Should I tell them about my sensory issues?
2. When do I tell them about my sensory issues?

3. How do I tell them about my sensory issues?

4. What if they hate me because I'm different?

5. What if they like me and invite me to places I can't go?

6. What if they like me and don't invite me anywhere?

7. What if they like me and want to spend time with me but I need space?

8. What if no one wants to be my friend?

9. What does all this say about who I am?

Because I'm moving toward that mystical place in my life where I just don't care what people think anymore (it's in the distance, but I see it coming), I can answer these questions differently than I would've at your age.

1. *Should I tell them about my sensory issues?* Yes, if this person is ever going to be a real friend, they're going to need to know the real you, not just the social media *'here's what I'd be if I were a unicorn-stuntman-billionaire-fairy-person-hybrid'* you. I like to think of it as a great measuring stick for whether a person is worthy of your friendship (how do you like that powerful thought?) If you think the person can't handle it, they're not going to make a good, supportive friend, and frankly, you can do much better.

2. *When do I tell them about my sensory issues?* Ugh, the act of disclosure. I still get freaked out about the "when" piece. It's big enough for people to know about sooner rather than later to avoid that awkwardness when they invite you somewhere you're super not ready to handle. I read a person when I meet them. First, I make the friend decision: *Yes, they'd be a good friend*, or *Absolutely not*. Then I move into letting them know. It's not the only important thing about me, much as it's not the only important thing about you. But it's a valuable piece of information, and again, someone who will end up being a good friend will not only be able to handle that information, but also be honored you shared it with them.

3. *How do I tell them about my sensory issues?* So many people, adults and teens alike, have asked me for my best one-liner on describing SPD. I usually say something like this: *Hey, can I tell you something important about me? I have a neurological difference called Sensory Processing Disorder, or SPD for short. It impacts the way I make sense of information from my senses, like sight and sound. Just wanted you to know in case it comes up. Feel free to ask questions about it. Because I'm typing and not*

speaking, it sounds weird and formal, so read this book, take those sentences, and make them your own. You might say, *I'm sensitive to things like sight, sound, touch, taste because I have a neurological difference/disorder/disability* (those three Ds are up to you; use one, all, or none). I like to wrap my description up in some celebratory stuff (*I'm a leading adult advocate and award-winning author of books on SPD*—that literally never stops being exciting), or maybe for you, it's *I'm so sensitive that I'm able to hear/see/smell/taste [insert some cool superpower that most neurotypicals don't have].* Tone is part of it, too. I've learned to be more casual about my disclosure, because I've worked for the last decade on self-acceptance—plus I've said it a bunch since then. It stops feeling scary the more you say it in front of decent, understanding people.

4. *What if they hate me because I'm different?* Screw them. If anyone hates you because of who you are, that's their problem and not yours. Run, don't walk, in the other direction. I guarantee you'll find someone else over there who's eager to be your friend.

5. *What if they like me and invite me to places I can't go?*
This is a tough one. Say your friends are all going out to
the movies tonight, but you're not comfortable enough
with the bright screen, loud sounds, and humming audience to go. How do you feel staying behind? In my
experience, I've always felt ashamed and embarrassed of
my differences when I'm left out because of the things
I'm not comfortable doing. Scratch that. That's too kind.
Before I was diagnosed with SPD, I loathed myself each
time I couldn't figure out how to participate in a social
event. It made my guts hurt knowing people I really liked
were out in the world having fun without me. It still feels
that way, even as an adult, although my guts hurt less and
I don't hate myself for the things I'm not comfortable doing. But it doesn't make it any easier. You can try to join
them and see if you can modify the situation to better suit
your needs. Ask if you can see a movie at a different time,
pick a theater you know, or suggest going out for dinner
first at a familiar place and then heading home while the
group continues on. It's part of the reason I'm usually the
one planning social events. If I have some control over the
location and timing, I can find a way to participate more

comfortably. If you can't, and your only choice is to live with staying behind, try not to beat yourself up too much. There's always going to be another event. Maybe next time, you can help plan so you can be comfortable, too.

6. **What if they like me and don't invite me anywhere?** In a perfect world, I'd be invited to everything and required to attend nothing. If you're not invited and you think it's because of your sensory issues, talk to someone. If these people are actually your friends, someone will care that you feel badly. Maybe they don't want to make your life harder and they think by leaving you out, you won't have to make a decision about going somewhere that might make you uncomfortable. If no one cares, they're not really your friends. See #4.

7. **What if they like me and want to spend time with me but I need space?** All people need space. If you think you can't handle a social event, let them know. You don't always have to point at your sensory differences. You could say you're having a rough week and have too much homework to do. But you could also tell them the truth: *I need a break tonight, but let's hang out on Sunday* or whatever. Take your sensory siesta. You deserve to rest.

8. *What if no one wants to be my friend?* We have all been lonely and friendless at one point or another in our lives. Someone out there loves you, though: your mom, your cat, the lead singer of your favorite band who clearly sings with you in mind. I want to be your friend. I know on those friendless days, you feel worthless and sad, but I also know that those days pass and those feelings are temporary. It's going to get better.

9. *What does all of this say about who I am?* It says you're a person. You matter. The end.

The Takeaway

Having sensory issues doesn't mean you don't deserve to have friends. Sometimes it's hard engaging with them the way you'd like, but the good friends—the smart, decent people around you—will make an effort to understand and love you exactly as you are. If you haven't met these people yet, that's okay. Remember, teenagehood is temporary and people do grow up. Maybe your best friends are out there, waiting in your first week of college or at your next job. Have patience. You're worthy.

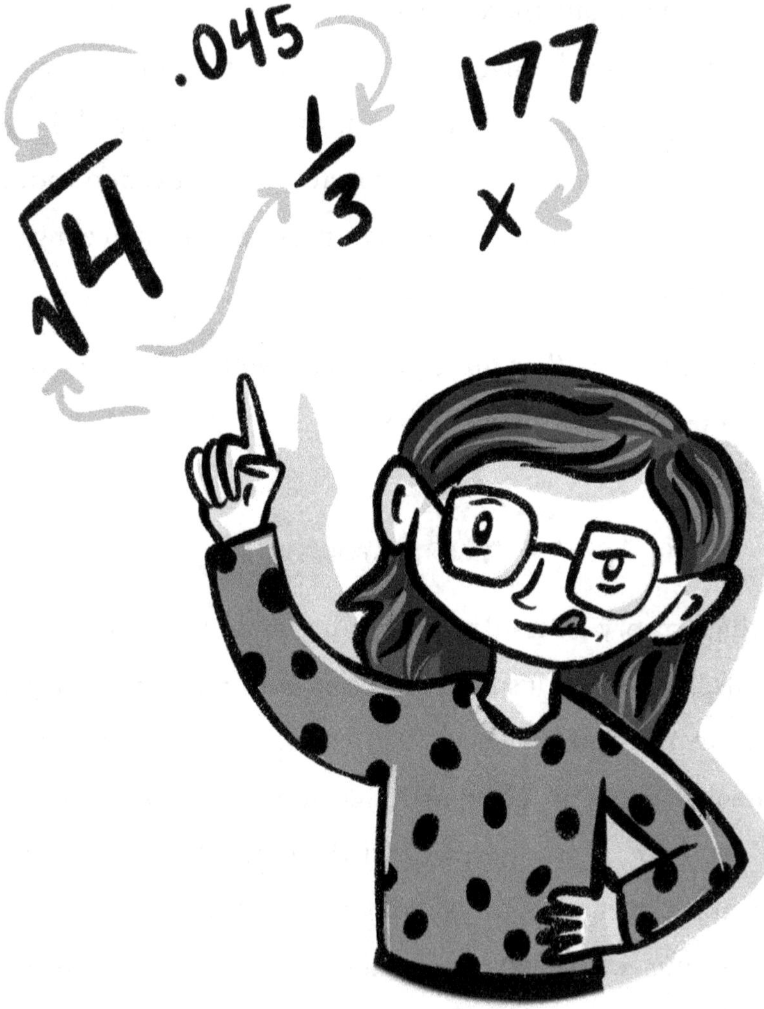
.045
177
x

CHAPTER 4
The Smart You: Academic Life

One of the biggest lies I ever told was back in third grade. Our teacher, a focused and driven woman named Mrs. Cantero, loved math, and it was her job to teach us our times tables. I remember feeling overwhelmed by the rows after rows of numbers and the thought that I had to memorize them. Words—those I could memorize. I was that genius preschooler who could actually read all by myself (I stunned my kindergarten teacher with my precocious reading abilities, so much so that I was handed over to the librarian for further instruction. No surprise: I became a writer and not a mathematician), but I've never been good at math. Ever.

In third grade, we had to learn our times tables, and I was struggling. Each week, we had to recite a times table to Mrs. Cantero in front of the whole class. If we succeeded, she'd give us a colorful smiley face in our notebook. If we failed, we didn't get a sticker and had to come back the next week and try again. I lived for those stickers and in fear of having to present those tables. They made no sense to me. One week, I stood up to recite what I knew would be some incomplete version of the eight times table, but Mrs. Cantero checked her grade book and said, "It looks like you've already done the eight times table, as well as the six and seven," and she told me I could sit back down. I said, "Oh, sorry!" My face red, the lights glaring, I knew she was wrong; I didn't know the six, seven, or eight times table. While she taught them to us, I'd been busy staring at our self-portraits lining the walls. I hadn't recited them at all, but I knew I'd gotten away with something big.

That was until fourth grade, when I still didn't know those times tables, and quickly fell behind the class in math. My teacher, Mrs. Tate, was kind and gentle, and she could see I was struggling. At lunch, when the other kids pulled out their sandwiches and sushi, she walked me down the hall for private tutoring. Each time we sat down together to review my work, I cried, because I was embarrassed, because I was called the Teacher's Pet for taking the beloved Mrs. Tate away from the class, and because math made absolutely no sense to me. Zero—the one math concept I understood.

In sixth grade, Ms. Lin passed around a stack of graded math tests. I'd scored a 60%, the lowest grade in the class and the worst grade I had in any class that year. Sensitive and quick to cry, as every report card ever sent home to my parents noted, I wept heaving tears in front of the whole class until Ms. Lin asked my friend to walk me out to the hallway to the fountain for a sip of water.

And then in late high school, I met Mrs. Thomas. She was a tiny little English woman who somehow always had command of our entire rowdy class. She saw me hunched over my quadrille notebook looking anxious and lost, and without making a big deal about it, she helped me. She broke down each math problem into a hundred little steps, which I wrote down line-by-line. I started sticking around after class to ask her casual questions that turned into mini lessons. I started showing up to class a little bit early to run my homework by her. She was patient and understanding, and she didn't make a big deal about my numerical struggles. It was like tutoring without the title and related emotions. Soon, I started sharing personal things with her too: my latest romantic crushes and conquests, my thoughts about college. We became friends. Photos from graduation day show us deep in conversation about my newest boyfriend. I emailed her once from college, letting her know that I had petitioned the Psych Department to let me take pre-calculus instead of calculus, and that I had a tutor. She was proud of me. (I got a C in that pre-calculus class, and I've never worked harder.)

To this day, my family calls my mathematical abilities *Sky Math*, as in *Rachel needs to draw numbers in the air with her fingers to do any math*. As in *Rachel does her math in the sky*.

* * * * * * * * * * * *

As much as I felt like a failure at math in high school, I knew I was gifted in English. While I hung around the math department looking for Mrs. Thomas' guidance, I spent most of my free time in the English department because it felt like home. The quirky cast of characters included sarcastic and dark-humored Mr. Benson, dramatic Ms. Keane and her infamous white bun, bright-eyed Mrs. Daniels who threw chalk at you if you didn't listen, and mild-mannered Mr. Closs. I adored them. In their company, I fell in love with both authors and poets. I've always loved reading and I always wanted to write, and it was in my high school English classes that I realized the impact that famous words had on my life.

If I felt scared, I said:
Things fall apart; the center cannot hold;
Mere anarchy is loosed upon the world.

If I was in love, I thought:
Love at the lips was touch
As sweet as I could bear
And once that seemed too much;
I lived on air.

When I was heartbroken, I scribbled:
Desire to us was like a double death.

In English class, I learned that words pulse through my veins. I devoured Sandra Cisneros' *The House on Mango Street*, J.D. Salinger's *The Catcher in the Rye*, and F. Scott Fitzgerald's *The Great Gatsby*. I honestly believed I was Catherine and my first love was Heathcliff, just like in Emily Brontë's *Wuthering Heights*. To me, books were the exploration of emotions—something that has always come naturally to me. I loved the chance to explore them even more through my own writing. While my classmates grunted and groaned when Mrs. Daniels assigned us essays, I quietly cheered as I noted the due date in my assignment book. Any chance to write, even to discuss the writing of others, was good enough for me.

But there was one assignment that I liked the most. Such a nerdy thing to remember so many years later. It was my final piece of writing in high school for Mr. Benson's class, and it was a *pastiche*, a work that imitates the style of another writer. I chose a Polish Jewish author named Bruno Schulz, whose vivid, richly worded style was unlike anything I'd ever read. I wrote a short story of a young girl going out from an event into the New York City night to lock the door to her apartment, which she had forgotten to do, and how she got joyfully lost along the way. It was the opposite of how I felt in my own life: scared, most of the time, to leave my apartment especially at night, but it was nice to pretend.

My favorite part was this:

A simple subway staircase emerged behind a slender signpost. Descending the stairs, I could hear the sound of the rhythmic, clicking turnstiles against the intense humming of subway trains that whirled through the underground tunnels. A six train opened its metallic mouth to me, revealing its teeth of sickly plastic chairs. I stood there, between the station and the train, curiosity rooting my feet to the floor. In one of the corners of the subway car, there may stand a man, placid and hushed, just turned twenty. He might lift his eyes to meet my gaze—violently blue eyes, fiery, imminent—trapped in his own cycle of contemplation and triumph and need. He was not there, and I rode the swaying car, feeling the absence of his presence that might not have existed outside of my mind. At the next stop, the train doors split open, ripped apart to observe my departure into the hollowed station, echoes of footsteps upon the already greyed tiles, flecked with bits of fallen stars.

I got the highest score possible from the dry-witted Mr. Benson. To this day, it's one of the most beautiful things I've ever written.

School Dazed

Okay, be honest. No one is watching. I'm only silently judging you. Do you hate school? Do you love it? Do you feel like your whole day is filled with highs and lows? Does it feel exhausting and overwhelming?

I don't think there's a right answer here, by the way. I know lots of sensory adults who loved school as teens—or parts of it anyway, and people who hated school and always felt like academic failures. Same goes for neurotypical people, too. The difference, once again, is the reason I'm writing this book; our experiences as sensory teens are different, and our sensitivities impact how we learn.

School can be hard. Some days, we spend more time in school than at home. It's a place where the things we love and the things we hate collide. If you're undiagnosed and unaware of your sensory differences, your classrooms could feel like the enemy without any reason. If you're aware of your SPD, you once again have to make that big decision: tell people or hide it. Maybe you tell your teachers but not your friends. Maybe your teachers have no idea. Telling your teachers probably means accommodations, like testing environments that fit your particular mix of sensory needs, but telling your teachers also means you're treated differently, and maybe others will notice.

The big problem is school classrooms are not usually designed for people with sensory issues. Lit with bright fluorescent lights and lined with reflective plastic floors, it's hard enough to learn algebra without hallway noise, the clicking pen next to you, the shifting room temperature, and your body's inability to figure out where the hell it is in space. Our eight senses (and our own unique blend of sensory differences) mean we have to work through extra layers before we even get to the challenge of learning. Add onto that the social piece of being at school all day with people you love/hate depending on the hour who may or may not understand your sensory needs, and yeah, school can be rough.

The funny thing is school can also be amazing for people with sensory issues. Many of us are considered gifted, especially in one or more particular areas, and there are now special schools for "twice exceptional" students. Are you a brilliant cello player and love music class? Do you practically live in the science lab? Do you haunt the English department like I did? I bet you're amazing at something—maybe even more so than your neurotypical friends. Thanks, sensory differences!

How to Strategize at School

At the end of the day (start your eye-roll now), high school is ultimately about learning and doing well enough to graduate, especially if you want to go to college. I know and you know that you're not going to use half of the things you learn in school in your adult life. The overly complicated math steps that Mrs. Thomas helped me break down? I never, ever think about them. Like I said, Sky Math all the way, baby. But I did become a writer, and the books I read in English class did have an impact on how I write. Something you're doing at school is going to influence your life as a grown-up, even if it's not as concrete as a formula or a book. It might be the way you learn to think about solving problems or how you work on a team project (or even lead the team—hello, future business executive).

What can you do so you can feel as comfortable as possible in school? How can you put aside your sensory differences so you can focus and do your best? These are the real issues here. I think it can be a two-part strategy:

1. *Consider telling your teachers.*

   Their job is to help you succeed. They don't want you to fail. They don't want you to struggle. If you don't have an IEP (see below), it still might be worth letting your teachers know about your sensory issues. The only experience I have with this is in grad school, because as you already know, I was 27 when I learned about my SPD. I let my professors know that I was distracted when every single fluorescent light was switched on in the classroom.

I told them I'd need to take breaks sometimes to use my Wilbarger brush and to have some quiet time. Most teachers didn't mind relying on natural light or giving the class a five-minute pause every once in a while.

2. *Try to use your tools.*

Some professors didn't particularly care about my sensitivities. I get it, I was one of many, but I still had to be comfortable in the classroom. Before I really knew where to find sensory tools, I was creating my own to meet my needs. This led me to wearing big, silly, blue-tinted aviator sunglasses in the classroom. I looked like a 1970s TV cop, but by wearing them, I didn't care if the professor insisted that every fluorescent light stay on. They helped soften my visual field. People walking by our classroom would actually stop and stare at me, because again, who wears blue-tinted aviator sunglasses indoors-slash-ever? Me, the fashion queen, that's who.

What are your favorite sensory tools to help you focus? Can you use any of them at school? I'm always thinking about ways to "grow up" kids' sensory tools. So maybe instead of fidgeting with putty or a colorful plastic tangle, you can play with a pen cap or nubby eraser. If you like weight on your lap but don't feel happy about a lap pad in public, can you put your bag or backpack on your lap? Or maybe a textbook? Ask your friends for hand squeezes when you need some input and keep a cold bottle of water around. I'm not sure why I feel better knowing I have access to one, but I do.

How about an IEP?

Full disclosure, when I see "IEP," I read it as "eye-EEEE-p," so that's something. And if you haven't heard of it, that's totally fine. I'm only starting to learn about it, too. It's an Individualized Education Plan (get it, I-E-P), and its job is to help you manage any learning differences while prepping you for life after school. From what I gather, even high school seniors can apply to participate.

Will it help you succeed in school? I can't say for sure, but I might've been better at math if I had asked for accommodations. If you have one, rock it! If you don't have one, maybe look into it?

Side Note

I should mention that, despite my challenges with math, I was an excellent student. I went to an international school, and instead of Advanced Placement classes, we had something called the International Baccalaureate program, or the IB program. With three college-level courses and three advanced-placement-level courses, I did such advanced work that I got to skip a whole year of college. Take that, sensory differences.

CHAPTER 5
The Home You: Family Life

To this day, I am most myself at home, especially when I'm surrounded by my original family. *The Unit*, as we still so cleverly call ourselves, consists of my parents, my younger sister, and me, although we've expanded since childhood with one adored brother-in-law and three gorgeous children, one of which is mine by birth, two of which are mine by the power of auntly love.

But back when I was a kid, before life got super real as it does in adulthood, there were four of us. In many ways, we were a "perfect" family because we loved being around each other so much. We're still incredibly close. Both of my parents worked, but my mom was always home to meet me and my sister after school for a snack and a chat in our kitchen overlooking the tall buildings of New York City. My dad would come home for dinner, and the four of us would always eat together, sharing stories of our days at school and at work. As a young kid, I knew the names of my parents' work clients as much as they knew the names of my friends and teachers.

My parents had a little house in what we called "the country," and on the weekend, we'd escape to our own little getaway spot. My sister and I would ride our bikes up and down the driveway in spring, run through the sprinklers in summer, sled down the hill out back in winter, and cut jack-o'-lanterns in the fall while my mom toasted pumpkin seeds for nibbling. On snowy afternoons, my dad would pop enough popcorn to feed a small village. We'd each get our own bowl, and we'd watch a movie together on the couch. It was always the four of us. The Unit.

We did fun away-from-home things together too. Museums, day trips, apple and pumpkin picking, lots of shopping—nothing crazy (only one of us has ever jumped out of an airplane; I live my most colorful life through my adventurous sister), but we often had plans. I just didn't understand why plans were hard for me. I loved the feeling after plans, when we came back home or to the country house, tired but having experienced something, and free to just rest until dinner time. But it was before the plans—waiting on the activities—that I felt scared and uncertain.

I can't say when it happened, but somewhere along the way, my dad became my safest person—my *Handler*, as I'd call him these days, or anyone who helps a sensory person navigate the world, even though I felt safe with each member of my family. He was the person who knew how to best remove me from an uncomfortable situation and whisk me to safety. I'm guessing it's because he was our family's one driver, and because he's always been tall and strong, a steady physical presence when the physical world felt icky.

Not every outing ended with me needing to be walked or driven to safety, but as I moved into my teenage years post-Canada and post-puppet, it happened much more often. Part of it was because I was so afraid I would have another episode that I did. My fear of the thing I had that I couldn't explain made everything we did especially scary. I didn't know when I'd lose touch with the world around me, so trips to the mall with my family became *trips to the mall that could end badly*. Apple and pumpkin picking became *apple and pumpkin picking, but what if I didn't feel well?*

And that was a big part of it. I knew each time I had one of my unusual episodes (again, what we wrongly called "panic attacks" at the time), I was impacting my family. One summer, sometime after Canada, we were in Boston during the Fourth of July weekend. We had made plans to have a seafood dinner at a restaurant first before walking through the bright streets in the sweaty early evening to find a place to watch the fireworks. I want to say our plans were to watch from a bridge, which makes me laugh now, because nothing sounds worse to me than watching fireworks from a strange, packed bridge in an unfamiliar city on a July night. But there we were again: nighttime, after dinner, summertime. I can't say if it was the memory of the marionette or the way sounds and sights blur together in the summer outdoors at night before sunset, but walking in the middle of a moving crowd, I once again lost my connection to everything. Sights and sounds were sharp and painful, I felt stuck inside my body. All that was missing was a weird puppeteer shouting French at me.

I said, "I don't feel good," that barely English phrase that let my parents know what was happening, and they steered me to a little metal table and chairs on the side of the street and sat me down. With my head in my hands, I remember feeling embarrassed and ashamed, but mostly very aware of the impact I was having on the people I loved the most. Through the disconnect I remember thinking: *They're going to miss the fireworks because of me and the things that are wrong with me.* Fireworks: the once-a-year treat we used to watch from the roof of our New York City apartment building, just a few blocks away from the river and the barge of colorful explosives. The thing we always saw together, arm-in-arm. I knew my family loved those fireworks as much as I was growing to hate them, but the thought of taking them away from my parents and sister made my stomach hurt.

And at the same time, I knew I had no choice. I knew as I sat at that strange table with crowds of people flowing past us looking at me strangely that in a few more moments, my dad would help me stand up and I would put my arm through his. I knew he would become my eyes and ears as he guided my lost body safely through the streets of Boston until we were back in the quiet of our hotel room, the fireworks blinking flat on the TV screen. Me, trying to cry quietly in the bathroom so I wouldn't upset my parents and sister. My family, loving me anyhow.

* * * * * * * * * * * *

Confession: this chapter is the hardest for me to write. I actually saved it to write last because I wasn't sure what to say or how to say it. Mostly because I don't want my family thinking, for a single second, that they didn't do the right things for me as a kid, teen, or young adult. To this day, they each still do their very best to make sure I'm heard, supported, and comfortable. Sometimes they kick me in the butt; no one does this more effectively than my mom, who sees better than anyone the big things I'm capable of doing, even when I'm too overwhelmed to see it myself. They're the people who taught me, so many years before I learned I had sensory differences, to push my limits. At the time, I didn't understand what those limits were or how to move smoothly around them, but at my family's insistence, I kept throwing myself against my boundaries. Sometimes, I pushed too far (see: Canada at night, Boston at night), but sometimes I was successful.

When I told my family about my diagnosis of SPD at age 27, it took them a little while to get comfortable with the new information and what it meant. I'm sure it brought up their own uncertainty and the times I struggled as they searched for an-swers. But the more we talked about it and the more I shared with them the ways that I perceive the sensory world, the more they read, and the better we all felt. Coming to terms with my sensory differences wasn't just something I did alone. My family also had to come to terms with my sensory differences and what it meant to be them if I was me.

Family Matters

I don't care how you feel about your family; your family matters.

And okay, I *do* actually *care* how you feel about your family. I hope you have loving, supportive parents, stepparents, siblings, grandparents, aunts, uncles, and cousins. I hope you have at least one person in your life who feels parental that you can turn to, especially in times of need, and friends or cousins who feel like sisters and brothers to hold your hand. But also, your family does matter, whoever happens to be in your circle.

I know families are complicated and adding sensory differences makes them even more so. Over the last decade, I've heard a few horror stories of parents denying their teens of their sensory differences (one, which I won't share word-for-word, involved a mom actually making fun of her teenage son—this told to me personally by the son—and made my skin burn with anger). But the good news is these stories aren't told very often, and instead I hear from lots of teens' parents who just want to help and support their kid. I also hear from lots of you about how your parents want to support you.

Either way, it's complicated to be a teen with sensory differences and be part of a family. Maybe like me, you feel that your challenges and needs upset the fun things your family wants to do together. Maybe you feel your siblings are frustrated because you get more attention and need more support. Maybe you feel like everyone gets it and things are great. Maybe you'd rather hide away from your family in the safety of your bedroom and feel really disconnected from them. Maybe they accept you. Maybe they don't.

Part of what makes it complicated is the stage of life you're in. As a teen, you start to own your SPD for the first time. As a kid, if you knew you had differences, it was likely your parents or guardians who took on the role of ownership because you were too little to know the difference. *Oh, little Timmy's senses are overloaded again? Let's turn off the music,* your mom might have said. But now it's all you, baby—or, well, it's mostly you. You're still in that middle-of-the-road phase where you're not a kid and not an adult. So you're probably learning to own your sensory differences for the first time. If you've known about your SPD since you were little, your parents are probably learning how to let you take ownership. Instead of jumping in to describe your needs, they might be taking a step back to let you speak up instead. They might also still be stepping in and speaking for you, which I'm guessing could feel frustrating, since it's your turn to do this now.

Whatever the case, my best guidance is to always talk about it. Put aside any big feelings and talk about what you're seeing and what you'd like to happen.

If you feel like they're speaking for you, maybe try saying something like:

Thanks, Dad, for wanting to talk to my science teacher about the problem I'm having with the classroom light, but I'd like to try telling him first. Is it okay if I call you in after if I still need help?

If you feel like you need more support, perhaps try saying something like:

I don't know how to explain why going out to dinner is hard for me to Aunt Penny. Can you help me figure out what words I can use? Can you be on the phone with me when I call her?

What I know for sure is that your family loves you, however your unit is structured. They want to see you grow, they want to see you succeed, and they want to have the chance to cheer you on. From what I've seen, sensory parents are always looking for the best, most effective ways to make your life more comfortable. The more you can explain your needs to them, the better your life will be.

Just don't forget to thank them for their help and support. Letting them know they're making a difference makes all the difference.

CHAPTER 6
The Bae You: Romantic Life

There's so much I want to teach you about dating as a sensory teen, but to understand what I've learned, you first need to know how I learned it.

With that, let me introduce the boys.

Nico

His name was Nico, and he gave me butterflies. Except his name wasn't Nico. But the butterflies were true.

I met him at camp, down by the lake where we took the campers boating. He was shy and kind with a sweet smile, and I thought that for a boy from the city, it was nice that he knew how to row a boat. It sounds silly now; I was barely 14, but I liked him and it was that simple. He's the one who presented me with the necklace on the hill that magical/awful summer of the marionette. He was my first boyfriend, the other half of my first kiss after seeing *Romeo and Juliet* (I kissed him and he stood there—oh, the romance), and writer of my first-ever love letter, which I snuck away from my campers to read.

He was my first representation of safety in a non-family member. I never really felt safe in my body, so it felt good to have someone on the outside of me to turn to as my safety net. If my feelings felt too big and overwhelming and my body felt uncomfortable, at least someone could hold my heart for a while. It's less scary when someone sits with you in your feelings. Nico was the first of many guys to sit with me in my feelings.

Nico's younger sister hated me. She taunted me and tortured me. She once blamed me for an asthma attack, gasping and sputtering as I stood by helplessly. Me, the nice girl. I'd like to say I didn't care, but you already know I did. She didn't break us up. I actually don't remember why we broke up, only that my dad drove me to Nico's house so he and I could work things out or end things properly. He sat in a chair next to his bedside lamp. I remember shadows, the light. Lots of crying. And then it was over. I gathered up everything that reminded me of him and put it in a driftwood box that looked as if it'd been flung from the Titanic. My first Boyfriend Box. Nico may not have been my first love, but he was still my first boyfriend, and each guy that followed him would also get his own box.

They're in storage somewhere in my parents' attic—proof to a future, older me that even as a teenager, I was once someone worth loving. (As are you.)

James

His name was James, and I was so in love with him that my skin hurt. Except his name wasn't James. But the skin part was true.

I was all of 15 years old and I hadn't given him a second thought, even though he teased me about bringing a purple umbrella on a walk through the woods in camp on a barely drizzly day. Even though we made s'mores. Even though he was tan from the summer sun and brooding and had eyes the color of freshly brewed coffee. He was off-limits, a dear friend's cast-off. And besides, I was busy navigating the end of my first relationship with Nico. I didn't notice when James called nightly. It didn't occur to me when he left a present for me with my building's doorman. Why would anyone be interested in me? I was still that same sweet, sensitive, nerdy girl who had meaningful conversations with her turtle in the safety of her own bedroom.

It took a mixtape for me to pay attention. James handed me my first one in late summer. We sat across from one another

24 flights up on my parents' terrace. In his arms was my father's guitar, which he strummed as he hummed Radiohead. I opened the thin plastic box of the tape to find a note, which I copied that night word-for-word into my diary, and still have to this day. It essentially asked: would I give him a chance? He'd asked me that same question for nearly a year—in the woods and over s'mores and in a note left with that present. I don't know why it took the mixtape for me to hear him and see him and to realize he heard and saw me. Had he always had a beauty mark on his forearm? Did his ears always stick out sweetly? Was he always so tall and were his shoulders always so broad?

When he left that night, I closed the door to our apartment and sprawled out on the carpet, snow-angel style, limbs stretched. The room spun. Looking back, I'd say I'd "hit the deck"—my favorite sensory term for how I use the supportive security of the floor to reconnect me to my body. And I needed to be reconnected. In a single afternoon, I'd somehow risen above my body to a plane I'd never been before. "It's love, isn't it?" my mom said, standing over me with a small smile.

Yes, it was. First love, the best kind. He called me Starshine and wrote songs about me filled with images of constellations and light. I loved his songs as much as I loved him. When he presented me with music and lyrics, I presented him with poetry, and back and forth we went, inspiring each other. We put stars up on my ceiling and picked two that were his for me to wish on every night. And every night I wished that I was just a little bit older and we could dream under them together.

It was the sort of love I hope you all get to experience at least once: like catching on fire and being so mesmerized by the bright beauty and the warmth that you don't realize you're being burned alive by the flames. Was I in pain or was I glowing? It changed from day to day, from minute to minute.

When things were good, we were busy kissing. He was so tall that I felt small and protected next to him, and I felt especially safe as we kissed our way around New York City. We kissed at the New York Aquarium behind dimly lit tanks of colorful fish. We kissed at the top of a mountain of rocks in Central Park. We kissed in coffee shops. We kissed in the stairway of my apartment building. But mostly, we kissed 33 flights up on the apartment building's roof, surrounded by skyscrapers. It's the roof that I remember most. We weren't supposed to be there; my parents and the landlord would've all agreed on that, but we didn't care. I felt safe there, high above and far away from the noise and motion of the city below. It felt like everyone could see us and no one could see us all at once. It was like the universe had hands and we were sitting together in one palm.

When things weren't good, we yelled at each other over the phone. He said I talked to too many other boys. He didn't get to see me enough. I was too busy. I must still like Nico. He pushed, poked, and prodded at me. I felt scared, insecure, and insignificant. I felt unloved and unsafe. This made my anxiety worse, which made my very much undiagnosed sensory sensitivities heighten.

When things weren't good, I spent a lot of time crying. I'd sit for hours trying to figure out what I'd done wrong. I was so sensitive that I read deeply into his absences. I didn't know then that was just who he was: present until I got too close to him (or was it that he got too scared of losing me? I'm still not sure) and he'd push me away. It was a cycle, like with his music and my poetry. And around and around we went.

I spent the day after my Sweet 16 crying. James had spun some tale about hanging out with a close female friend of mine to make me jealous, and it marked the end of our short, deep five-and-a-half months together. As a grown-up looking back, I want to be like: *Hey, Rachel, you don't deserve to spend the day after your big, special party in emotional agony. No one should make you feel that small, no matter how intensely you love them.* But as a teen, I felt like most people spent many days crying about love, and I just happened to be one of them. And I guess, actually, we all do, at all ages, whether or not we deserve it. We cry for the ones we love, especially when we can't find a way to love them and be loved by them. It's why first loves linger long after they're gone.

Nate

His name was Nate, and I liked watching him from a distance. Except his name wasn't Nate. But the distance-watching thing was true.

I spotted him before I knew him, down a grassy hill near the basketball courts where he taught campers how to climb the ropes course. You could say I had a crush on his baseball cap. That sounds about as ridiculous as it was. It was white and he had dark hair, and I saw him in his khaki cargo shorts and baseball cap and thought he was cute. From where he stood, he could look up the hill to the picnic table that was assigned to my camp group. We may have appeared tiny to one another, but I liked that we could always see each other.

Nate was stable, honest, and sweet. He called me Kitty Cat, and his physical presence brought me peace, especially after the burning fireworks factory that was James. Twenty years later, with the clarity that comes with being a grown-up, I can tell you that he loved me in a very accepting, honest way. It's why, at 17, we dated for over a year.

Outside of camp, we spent time at each other's apartments across town from one another. I didn't like to go out on dates, and my anxiety and other unexplained sensitivities (my undiagnosed SPD—let's call it what it was) kept me from major adventures in the big city. Really, getting from my apartment to Nate's was an adventure itself. On a bold day, I took three buses, even though taking the subway would've been quicker (I always felt stuck and scared on the subway). On uneasy days, when I felt like I'd lose my increasingly delicate connection to the physical world around me, my parents would treat me to a taxi. Again, these were days before smartphones and apps (and Uber), and I'd sit for the entire ride, clutching dollar bills and trying to do Sky Math to add the right tip to the amount on the meter. By the time I got to the Upper West Side, I was dizzy, drained, and in need of one of Nate's safe hugs. Safe—Nate made me feel safe.

Nate didn't mind that I wasn't as mobile as other girls—or he didn't seem to mind. The truth is we never talked about the things I could and couldn't do. I'm not sure why, but truly, even I didn't know what was going on inside me. Nate seemed to understand without words. Sometimes, we'd go for walks down the block to his neighborhood candy store, where he bought me dark chocolate-covered pretzels. Most of the time, we hung out in his apartment. We snuck in pizza and kissed on his futon. I have the vague sense that his mom was around sometimes, but never his dad, and the memories that stick years later place us in that apartment, entirely alone and curled up together.

We would've continued on and on, I suspect, had it not been for the dangerous boredom that sometimes come with repetition. He was so safe and so kind that I stupidly looked up and right into the eyes of his best friend, Enzo.

Enzo

His name was Enzo, and I thought he was exciting. Except his name wasn't Enzo. But the exciting part was true.

He was Italian, born in Italy, and he had a beautiful accent. I don't know why I felt I needed a bridge away from Nate, but to me, Enzo was not just a bridge, but one lit up at night, laced with lights. I met him at my parents' house when Nate brought him over for a visit. I think Nate honestly wanted me to get to know his friends, but Enzo was dangerously tall (I have a type, I guess) and there was a spark of something alive in his eyes.

I was almost 18, but not quite, and a few years into therapy for my anxiety at this point. I think Enzo filled a unique need for me: he fed the pieces of me that were sensory-seeking. As you know, when someone with SPD is *dysregulated*, our system is unbalanced. We go from feeling neutral, calm, and organized (in a sensory way, in an emotional way) to wild extremes. We might go from avoiding a kind of sensory input to seeking it out. I wonder if this is why I've always had a pattern with boyfriends: calm, exciting, calm, exciting. Too much of one and I seek out the other. I can't say for sure, but Enzo was pure excitement.

Anyhow. The pain of ending things with Nate has been lost to time, but I know it was really big. I think I told him I liked someone else but didn't say who at first. Nate was furious when he found out that his girlfriend and best friend had betrayed him, and he made all sorts of threats that worried all sorts of authority figures.

But Enzo called me *bellisima* (beautiful) and *amore mio* (my love), and I swooned. There were flowers and love letters and kisses, and that was pretty much it—we had nothing but Nate in common. When it ended, I felt burnt out by the non-stop serious dating of all of these boys. Later, in my 20s, I'd call this hopping from boyfriend to boyfriend *lily-padding*, like the way a frog might leap from lily pad to lily pad. I've always been a lily-padder because, like I said, I always felt safest when a kind guy was helping me hold my heart.

I decided I wouldn't actively look for anyone else to date. I had little crushes here and there but nothing worth writing about.

And then my best guy friend at the time took me to the prom.

Tom

His name was Tom, and he was my best guy friend senior year. Except his name wasn't Tom. But the best guy friend part was true.

He was Australian, the son of a diplomat, a lover of dinosaurs and fossils, and the kindest and most sincere person I knew. We met in homeroom, where he gravitated toward a pair of best gal pals who were barely at the fringe of our grade's social circles. I can't remember when he shifted away from them and why, but by mid-senior year, we'd gone from saying hi in homeroom to spending excessive amounts of time together, baking Australian Anzac cookies and predicting the professional fates of our classmates.

Our senior prom was scheduled to take place on a private boat at night, and Tom and I planned on going together as friends. (Because that's how teens did prom in my day—no fancy asks, just a mutual shrug of *okay, let's do it.*) For many people, a dinnertime sail around the tip of Manhattan and past the Statue of Liberty sounds glamorous. For me, it was stomach-churning. You can't escape a boat once it's set sail, and not knowing that my urge to flee was motivated by sensory factors, it scared me to think I couldn't leave once we left port. But I knew Tom would be there, and Tom was gentle and safe.

On the night of the prom, I was nervous. But, wrapped up like a mermaid in an iridescent, shell-colored gown with long, flowing hair, even I knew I looked beautiful. Special. When Tom came to my parents' apartment to pick me up, he looked special too, all buttoned up in his tuxedo. From behind his back, he pulled out a box with a wrist corsage—three baby pink roses (my favorite flower) and silver string. My parents, having been notified of the surprise beforehand, ducked into their bedroom to retrieve a boutonniere for me to give Tom. As we posed for pictures, he wrapped his arms around me differently than usual, pulling me close. Tom, the Australian dino lover, my friend. I remember thinking, *Wait a second, what's happening here? Isn't this just your best male buddy decked out for a rite of passage? When did we get so cozy?* I quickly put those thoughts out of my mind. After all, I had a boat to deal with.

Tom and I walked along the dock and up the gangway as the sun set. Inside, we found our little quirky group of friends and picked out a table to sit at. The boat set sail, and as the rest of the senior class climbed stairs to the dance party already raging on the roof, Tom and I stayed behind. He took my hand and led me out to a small balcony over the water. It was fully dark by then; the only lights were those of the city skyline, bright and stunning, ahead of us. I didn't know if I should look out or at him. Neither option seemed as scary as I thought it'd be a few hours before. He didn't kiss me—in fact, we wouldn't talk about what happened that night until late the next day, after we walked across the stage of the General Assembly Hall of the United Nations, and officially graduated.

By dinner that night, we were a *We*. It felt equally strange and totally normal.

Tom called me "My Little Rach" for the two months leading up to college. I remember lying on his bed in his room in late summer, his younger sister popping in and out to tell us stories and make us laugh. He told me he had an idea: he'd stay in the US instead of heading back to Australia with his family in the fall. He'd work while I went to school. We'd be together. He told me he loved me. But I couldn't let him do that. I knew he couldn't—shouldn't—stay. I was 18, I wasn't ready for forever, and he had so much more to learn about the educational things he loved the most. I don't remember breaking up, but Tom did go back to Australia. Years later, he went on to get his PhD in something fancy related to dinosaurs, just as we predicted he would.

There are more of them. So many more, even before my teenage years were up. I could tell you about the really boring one I almost mistakenly married or the ones that followed. But when I think back to my undiagnosed teenage years, these are the guys that stand out. Each one, in his own way, held up a mirror to show me who I was and variations on who I could become. When I talk about people building your bones as you're living your life, I'm talking a great deal about these guys.

* * * * * * * * * * *

Dating Takeaways

Listen, I know that dating can seem scary when you have sensory differences. In dating, you have to expose enough of your personality, likes and dislikes, and history to a person to see if you're compatible. You have to be vulnerable. You have to be honest. You have to leave your bedroom. I think it's all of this plus having to explain your SPD to someone—and your worth beyond your differences—that keeps many teens and adults away from finding love. I've spoken to so many people over the last 10 years who tell me they're just not worthy of being loved. To them I say, *WRONG!* Everyone is worthy of being loved, whether you have sensory issues or are neurotypical, whether you're a teen or an adult. All people deserve love, period. But if you believe you don't deserve it, you won't find it.

Because I was an undiagnosed sensory teen, I couldn't explain my SPD to anyone, and while I knew I had anxiety and related challenges, I was always looking to be loved and adored. For me, dating was, as I'd learned with Nico, a way for someone to hold my heart and sit with me in my feelings. And I've always had very big feelings (a true perk of being so sensitive). A friend of mine recently pointed out that I've never really been without a boyfriend, and she's right. Once I saw how safe it felt for someone to accompany me as I carried my big feelings, I never wanted to be without that helper.

Also, what's not to love about love? I was hooked the second James looked into my eyes with something between recognition and desire. I wanted him to think about me as much as I thought about him. I wanted Nate to hold my hand and Enzo to call me romantic nicknames and Tom to see me a little more like a gorgeous mermaid and a little less like a friend.

So, What Now?

Am I supposed to teach you how to date? I'm not sure. My advice is to do what you feel is right. If you like someone and want to date them, try it. Ask them. Pick a spot to meet that you feel safe and comfortable in—someplace you've been before so you know what sensory input to expect. Choose a time of day that you feel your best. Be yourself. If someone doesn't like you purely because of your sensory issues, they're clearly not the right person for you. BYE, LOSER. I always say I don't want to be a part of any club that wouldn't want me as a member. The right person will love you with your SPD, because of your SPD, and just as you are. Remember, you're more than your differences and you're also amazing because of your differences. Good people know that.

And How about ... Errrmmm ... Ummm ...

Am I allowed to say *sex* in this book? Who knows? So, let's call it the super-mature term *errrmmm ... ummm.*

A short, embarrassing ERRRMMM ... UMMM Q&A with the author, Rachel

Q. Did you have *errrmmm ... ummm* as a teenager?

A. Yes, at 19, but I spent the five years leading up to it working my way toward it with the boys you just read about. Awk-ward.

✻ ✻ ✻

Q. Did your SPD get in the way?

A. I'm a very tactile-seeking, proprioception-unaware person, so not at all, but I do know lots of sensory people who avoid *errrmmm ... ummm* even in adulthood.

* * *

Q. What if my sensory needs keep me from *errrmmm ... ummm*?

A. Trust me, it's not the end of the world if you're not into it now. You're young, life is long, and you have plenty of time. There's also life outside of *errrmmm ... ummm*, but it's a pretty big thing to miss out on doing eventually. What sensory tools can you use to make it feel less—icky? Overwhelming? (I'm not sure exactly how it makes you feel.) Maybe break things down and see what pieces of *errrmmm ... ummm* feel best for you. Rock those pieces. It should be fun and not miserable.

* * *

Q. Should I run out and *errrmmm ... ummm* right now?

A. Oh god, do I have to make that call?! Please don't do that to me. No? Maybe? Whatever you do, be safe and careful—and don't force yourself to do anything that makes you uncomfortable from any perspective (sensory, emotional, physical, religious, etc.)

Hi, Mom and Dad. It's me, your grown daughter. This has been as awkward for me to write as I'm sure it feels for you to read. You're welcome and I'm sorry.

RACHEL

To summarize:

1. You're worthy of being loved.
2. You're capable of loving others.
3. Date if you want to date.
4. Don't date if you don't want to date.
5. Leave me out of the *errrmmm ... ummm* decisions.

CHAPTER 7
The Public You: Social Media Life

Disclaimer: maybe I'm not the right person to talk to you about social media. I was part of the first wave of colleges invited to use Facebook for the first time (one of the most amazing days of my life, by the way), but I had to google TikTok just now so I could write any of this coherently. How to phrase this: social media comes and goes so fast that you're already too old to talk to 'tweens about the next big thing, too. Whatever current 10-year-olds will be into in six years is going to confuse you, guaranteed.

So. As long as you're good with that, we can talk about social media and sensory issues, because regardless of your age and favorite social media platforms, something important happens to us with social media. Social media is this magical place where we can show people exactly what we want them to see about our lives. We tell the story we'd like to read about ourselves. Ignore the parts you hate, cut out the pieces that make you feel like a failure, airbrush that pimple out, and you're your very best self all of the time.

Then together, we pretend that what we're seeing and reading is real. To others, we're the funniest person ever. We're brilliant. We're talented. We're gorgeous. We're exactly that story as we wanted to tell it. And strangely, at the same time, we secretly believe we can't compare to the rest of the people we know. We're not brilliant enough. We're not talented enough. We're ugly. Doesn't matter if you're on Instagram, Snapchat, TikTok, Facebook—it's the same wherever you go.

Now add in a very sensitive person with sensory differences, maybe you. If you're pretending what you're seeing and reading is real, there's a very good chance that social media makes you feel like garbage and calls attention to your differences. Everywhere you look, someone is having the best weekend ever partying by a pool. Or hanging out in the city with their best friends. Or taking their perfect dog on a gorgeous hike in their beautiful but sporty clothes. Or being kissed by their boyfriend on their flawless-skinned cheek. Maybe you're scrolling from under your weighted blanket while fidgeting. Perhaps you're in a pair of noise-canceling headphones. Maybe you're recovering from a shutdown. Nothing like adding FOMO to SPD to make you feel the very worst.

* * * * * * * * * * *

Happy Media-um

A few questions to think about:

1. What story does your social media tell about you as a person?
2. How do you feel about the stories your friends' social media tell?
3. How do all these stories make you feel about yourself as a person with sensory differences?

Again, I didn't know I had SPD until I was a decade older than most of you. When the internet was brand-new, I was a whole dozen years old, and it doesn't look anything now like it did back then. I didn't have social media pressure during my teenage years and honestly, I don't envy any of you for it. It's hard enough being a teenager; it's extra hard being a sensory teenager, and it must be beyond hard being a sensory teenager with social media worries.

Do you ever let on about your SPD on social media? Do you use social media to rewrite some of the rougher spots in your differently wired life so you feel more in line with your neurotypical friends? Do you ever look at other people's accounts and wish your life was as glamorous, fun, and exciting as their accounts make it seem?

I post. A lot. Annoyingly, sometimes. And it's not about anyone else but my own feelings about myself and my imagined neurological shortcomings. *If I post a happy picture of this challenging event,* I think, *then maybe I'll believe it was easier for me than it really was.* Or even, *maybe others will forget about the things that make me sensitive and different.* Sometimes though, I post in celebration of an activity that was hard work for me, as simple as it looks and may feel to others, and sometimes I'm genuinely happy about what I'm seeing or experiencing, and I want to share it with the whole world.

I'm the last person to tell you to run screaming from social. I love crafting my image and telling my stories, whether or not they're 100% accurate every time. I like looking back at my accomplishments and my happy moments in spite of some challenging emotional and neurological packages I carry in this lifetime. However, if you feel you spend more time on social media comparing your life to others and beating yourself up for being different instead of sharing those happy moments, maybe you need to take a break. You're always going to have sensory differences. Using the (mostly made up) stories other people tell about their lives as another place to feel badly about yours won't change anything but your sense of wellbeing.

CHAPTER 8
The Professional You: Job Life

If you count babysitting, then I worked my first real job in my early 'tweens. Neighbors in our building needed someone to watch their kids for a few hours while they went out, and they asked mature and responsible me. Sadly, the kids and the neighbors are both nameless and faceless to me now so many years later, but I do remember the feel of hard-earned cash being pressed into my palm, and how it felt to unfold the bills in the elevator ride back upstairs and count the money. I'd never been so proud before. I learned right then and there that my time was valuable.

If you don't count the occasional babysitting gig, then my first real job takes us back to that magical summer by the lake. I was a counselor-in-training (CIT) and I'm pretty sure I wasn't being paid. But I was being treated more like an adult than I had before. Under the guidance of a sour-faced, rigid head counselor who managed to suck all of the fun out of camp, I accompanied a group of 9- and 10-year-old girls through their warm-weathered woodland adventures. Each day at 2 PM, CITs were let loose together for an hour of socializing (I suspect in exchange for not being paid). As you remember, I was new, and for the first week of camp, I didn't take a break because I was anxious about making friends with the other CITs. I knew I was a little bit quirky and sensitive, and having just finished 8th grade with pretty much no friends to speak of, I couldn't imagine anything would be different here. While my group of girls wove dream catchers in the art cabin, I sat on the porch during my break, pretending I loved sitting quietly alone. Even the head counselor looked at me strangely for being so anti-social. I didn't know how to explain my fears.

And then I met Louise. She was a new CIT like me—equal parts laid-back and enthusiastic, friendly but not overwhelmingly so, and she couldn't understand why she hadn't seen me on our breaks before. *But what do you do on your breaks?* she asked me, honestly confused about my sudden appearance in her life. When I couldn't figure out how to answer her, she said, *Never mind, next break you're coming with me. I have to introduce you to everyone.* Louise's "everyone" was, in fact, *everyone*—in a single round of introductions, I met the ladies who'd become some of my lifelong friends. I met my first boy-friend for the first time. I met my first love for the first time. They were all in the same place at once, the people who would build my bones.

The work, while technically my very first job, was sur-rounded by so many earth-shaking social firsts that I barely noticed the long hours in the summer sun. My anxiety decreased, and as the campgrounds and routine became familiar, my un-recognized sensory differences settled down as well. I know it doesn't say much about my work ethic (I swear, I have tons of work ethic), but I showed up every single day because I knew I'd have a full hour to spend with these very important people. Besides, it was fun being a counselor for the first time. The little girls looked up to me, and always the type to be an older-sister figure, I loved having the chance to teach them about the world.

If you don't count camp or babysitting, then I worked a few unpaid internships in my first summer home after my fresh-man year of college. But my first job—my first post-college, in-the-real-world job—was as a preschool teacher at a fancy New York City private school. I was 21, which is technically beyond the reach of this little book, and I *still* didn't know

I had SPD, but it was there, among the pandemonium only two- and three-year-olds can create, that I met the first person I ever knew with SPD. Strangely, I didn't know that Teddy's differences had a name, but I watched him go from calm and centered to overwhelmed and physically shaken in seconds. A special teacher would come in from time-to-time and wrap him up in blankets, help him dip his hands in sand, and give him squishy hugs.

I could've used some of those squishy hugs. My lead teacher was a snooty know-it-all who gave me looks when she left the room for a minute and a kid would cry. (Secret: sometimes children cry.) No matter how engaged I was with the kids, how often I made homemade playdough before she asked, or how gracefully I led snack time, I couldn't make her happy with me or my abilities to help care for her classroom. I'd hear her whispering things about me to the director of the program when she thought I wasn't in earshot. I started dreading going to work every day.

A few months into the noise, mess, and teacher drama, I lost my cool and ended up in a back bathroom angrily kicking a bag of diapers. It was then that I quit—just as the director asked me if I was willing to leave. To this day, I can't say if it was the sensory din created by a dozen young children or an unsupportive teammate who made me quit. But I still think of Teddy sometimes.

✳ ✳ ✳ ✳ ✳ ✳ ✳ ✳ ✳ ✳ ✳ ✳

Working It

Because I didn't know I had SPD when I worked as a teen, I didn't have the chance to understand the ways my sensory needs impacted how I like to work. What I learned from the preschool nightmare was that I wanted to work in a quiet, more controlled space—which I did, in an office, for many years (and now do, only remotely).

Whenever you start your work journey, it's very important to ask yourself questions about your ideal workplace and job. You have to be comfortable at work if you want to be good at what you do and not hate your daily life—and you deserve to be comfortable and happy.

Before looking for a job, ask yourself:

- What am I good at doing?
- What sensory input do I like?

- What sensory input do I hate?
- What job can I do that fits my needs?
- What job can I do that fits my skills?

If you're a person who feels terrible around loud, unexpected noise, maybe you shouldn't work summers at an amusement park. If you're someone who loves the tactile experience of petting animals, maybe you can walk neighborhood dogs. This idea can be applied to bigger, real-world, post-high-school and post-college jobs too. Most neurotypical people worry about finding a career they love that will pay them enough. Most sensory people worry about finding a career that they love that doesn't trigger their sensory issues and that also pays them enough. If you find a career that you love that soothes your sensory yucks and pays you enough, take it immediately. Those can be hard to find.

To Disclose or Not to Disclose

The first time I disclosed my SPD to a boss and team, I was, oh, 30. But again, that was only three years after finding out about my SPD. It took me some time to make sense of what my sensory differences meant in the workplace. At first, I was worried that if anyone found out I was different (or, in my head: *weird, challenged, quirky, picky, needy*), I would lose my job. These days, being let go from a job for having a difference/disorder/disability is not just frowned upon, but illegal. Because you're a teen, I won't overload you with too many details, but let's just say companies need to work with you and your differences, if your needs are reasonable. They can't fire you for your SPD unless your differences keep you from doing your job. If you're doing your work well, even with some slight need-based changes, you should be just fine.

Also, I like to think we're starting to live in an era of acceptance and celebration of what makes us unique. Companies are starting to really see how important it is to hire people with different backgrounds and different points of view. For these reasons, I want to encourage you to disclose your sensory differences to a boss – if you feel comfortable doing it, if you're able to do your job regardless of your sensory needs, and if the environment (and your boss) seems open to it.

You can say it like this. Feel free to change the words up so it sounds like you and not a grown-up author/advocate:

Hi [NAME], I was hoping to share something about my-self with you so you can understand a little bit more about me and how I work. I have Sensory Processing Disorder (SPD), a neurological difference that impacts how my brain makes sense of [ADD YOUR CHALLENGING SENSES HERE]. I wanted you to know because it means you might see me [TURN OFF EXTRA LIGHTS, USE A WEIGHTED LAP PAD, WEAR TINTED GLASSES, WEAR HEADPHONES, NEEDING A QUIET BREAK SOMETIMES—PICK SOMETHING TO PUT HERE]. But don't worry, I love my job and am so happy to be on your team. I'm glad to answer questions about it and send you some information [SEND THEM TO MY WEBSITE OR TO THE STAR INSTITUTE].

It's okay to be you, even at work.

RACHEL

To summarize:

- Think about your ideal workplace.
- Think about your ideal job.
- Think about your particular sensory challenges.
- Think about your skills.
- Find a job that work with your needs and skills.
- Disclose if you feel safe and able.
- Always be bold and befriend the people around you.

CHAPTER 9
Leaving High School

The months leading up to high school graduation, I was not-so-quietly freaking out about college. Mostly, I was worried about the unknowns: what would it be like to live away from home? How would I deal with unfamiliar people and places? Would they like me? How would I do with my classes? What would happen to my anxiety and my related episodes? All of it felt scary, but most of all, I worried about my roommate. One day in gym class, I looked sideways at some of the mean girls and thought: *What happens if I end up with a mean girl as a roommate?* I was quirky enough as it was. I didn't need a mean girl pointing it out to me 24/7 from the comfort of our shared bedroom.

Months later, after packing up my life and feeling like I was about to jump off a cliff into the unknown, I walked into my dorm room with my parents and way too many boxes. Half of the room was already taken and completely unpacked. It was simple and neat. Nothing stood out to me, except the massive Britney Spears posters smiling at me from across the room. (Not a fan of Britney over here, sorry.) I knew her name—Yang—and I knew she was from Hong Kong. But that was it.

Yang walked into our room, and I immediately felt her calm independence. Around her neck was her brand-new student ID. She'd already found the dining hall, the campus center, and the library. I briefly realized I wanted to be her in that moment and not emotional, frightened me.

When my parents said goodbye after a long day of un-packing, Yang grabbed my arm, and together we walked down our dorm hallway. I was exhausted from the big and necessary and sudden changes: my new room, my new state, my new life. But Yang took my arm anyhow and made me say hi to every-one. I met studious Rose and her hilarious roommate, Jennie. I met peppy Lara and her shy roommate, Kat. I met quiet Anne, who's still one of my very best friends.

Yang led us all to our first day freshman orientation activi-ties. She had the schedule memorized, and marching feet ahead of us, I felt a bit safer knowing she was there.

Late that night, tucked under the cloud-patterned sheets of my strange new bed, I felt anxious, sad, and alone. I heard

— Chapter 9 —

Yang get up and walk over to our dorm room's one window. It looked out into our echoey, buggy quad, which was basically a pit at the foot of the campus' best residence hall, an actual castle. The window was already wide open. It was late August in Boston and as hot as mid-summer.

Yang cleared her throat:

I want to make out! she shouted into the quad. Her voice bounced off of the surrounding buildings like a dozen Yangs chanting into the darkness. From under my covers, I giggled.

Then she shouted again:

I want to make out!

By then, I was rolling laughing, and so was she. For a moment, I forgot the sinking feeling of change in the middle of my stomach. Yang climbed back into her bed and we talked about life for a full hour before finally going to sleep.

A few days later, feeling overwhelmed and burnt-out from the transition into my new college life, I woke up crying. Yang took me to our Resident Advisor (RA)'s office and stood right outside the door like a guard-dog while RA Diana gave me a pep talk I still tell stories about to this day. Yang watched me closely for the next week, her mouth twisted into a worried knot.

I'd eventually choose to live with someone else the following year, hurting my first college friend's feelings in the process. I don't think I ever got to thank her for seeing me through one of the scariest transitions of my life. I definitely have never thanked her for not being one of the mean girls I worried about in high school gym class.

* * * * * * * * * * * *

The End is the Beginning

The end of high school is the beginning of a huge transition for you. Doesn't matter if it means college, your first job, or a year abroad: something is ending and something else is starting. People with sensory differences are great at lots of things, but transitions aren't one of them. We're usually the people who have trouble going from the supermarket to a street fair or from school to a restaurant. Those moments between the two secure places are often filled with the unknown, and we don't love the unknown, because it leaves lots of room for our senses to be surprised and overwhelmed.

This is one of those transitions, but on a grander scale. I know you're probably going, *Oh god no, why, Rachel? Why are you bringing this up? I don't want to know about this in advance!* I'm not here to upset you. Swear. But if I don't put it out there and point at it, it'll still happen to you and you'll be caught off guard.

My parents used to joke that I couldn't go to the University of Rachel's Bedroom. (I still swear I would've been a top student at URB, especially as the only student there and all.) You also can't go to the University of Your Safe Space or take that first post-high school job while swaddled in your comforter. To make progress, you have to move forward, too.

So, let's talk strategy.

RACHEL

We've already established that:

1. Change is tough, especially for people with sensory differences.
2. Change is necessary to move forward into adulthood (and yes, you have to grow up. Sorry, Peter Pan).

What else can you do?

1. *Make peace with change*

   See it, come to terms with it, and make room for it, as scary as that feels. The thing I need you to remember about this transition, regardless of what comes next for you is: you'll survive it—and then you'll love your new life on the other side. Or, well, hopefully you'll love it. If you don't, you'll make a new decision and transition into something else. The next piece of who you're about to become is happening thanks to the new things you'll learn, the people you'll meet, the places you'll live, and the things you'll do when you get there.

2. *Bring a piece of home with you*

   Sleep with your childhood stuffed giraffe? Comfiest in your worn pajama pants? Take them with you. Moving on into college or your first apartment and job doesn't mean you have to give up all of the familiar things you love. Ask your dad for his mac and cheese recipe and cook it for your suitemates. Introduce your coworkers to your favorite music. You're still you, even if it feels like You 2.0.

3. *Bring sensory tools with you*

You're going to need sensory tools more than ever. Yes, you may have to explain them to some new people, but do the things you need to do to feel your best during this time. See chapter 12 to read up on my favorite sensory treatment, tools, and techniques—and then use them.

4. *Take my RA's advice*

I can't tell you where my RA, Diana, even ended up. We lost touch years ago, and she'd probably be surprised to see such a significant shout-out in this book. But that day in her dorm room, she gave me advice that I still share in SPD presentations and use often. *Take it one second at a time. You only have to get through the first second to get to the next. Then take it one minute at a time, one hour at a time, one day at a time, until things feel better.* And they always feel better eventually. Even I stopped crying in the mornings and started living my college life as if it'd always been what I'd done.

Remember: transitions are temporary. New patterns turn into old patterns very quickly, and the once unfamiliar will feel familiar so soon. Have patience and try to see the joy of possibility.

CHAPTER 10

Advocating for Yourself

You may have noticed by now that I've started most chapters of this book with a personal story. I can't do that for this chapter because I never had to advocate for myself and my sensory differences in my teen years. I'd like to think I would have if I'd known what was going on, but I also know I could've told people about my (misdiagnosed) anxiety disorder, and I chose not to share. I was afraid the few people I had as friends would stop talking to me entirely. I wish I'd had more confidence in myself and the people who loved me.

What does it mean to "advocate" for yourself? It means to stand up for who you are by letting the people around you know what you need. It means sharing your story, challenges, and strengths with family, friends, and teachers. Mostly, it means accepting yourself as you are. If you don't accept yourself, how can you expect anyone else to?

How to go about this will probably be different for you than for someone else. Ask yourself:

- What do I want/need people to understand about me and my sensory differences?
- How do I want to be treated? Is it different from how I'm being treated now?
- Where should I speak up: at home? At school? With friends?
- What should I say?

Before you can advocate for yourself, you need to learn as much as you can about your sensory differences so you can teach people what they need to know. I'd say read a book, but if you've made it this far into this book, you've already done that—so, well done, you! Google things. Find scientific studies (google "SPD + UCSF + Dr. Elysa Marco") that you can send to people. Figure out the actual terms for the tools you use. SPD is real. The more educated you are about this, the more people will respect you and your sensory differences and believe you when you say, *This is what I need to feel my best.*

Some Words to Help You Start

I've already written some speeches for you throughout the book of ways you can begin your sensory-related advocacy convos with others, but I'm going to put them all here so you can easily pick and choose. My advice: use these as a place to start, and swap in your own words. Sound like yourself and not like an adult author; it's more real, and what you want most here is to be real and honest.

General/Social/School/Family

- *Hey, can I tell you something important about me? I have a neurological difference called Sensory Processing Disorder, or SPD for short. It impacts the way I make sense of information from my senses, like sight and sound. Just wanted you to know in case it comes up. Feel free to ask questions about it.*

- *I'm sensitive to things like sight, sound, touch, taste because I have a neurological difference/disorder/disability¬ (those three Ds are up to you—use one, all or none). I'm so sensitive that I'm able to hear/see/smell/taste [insert some cool superpower that most neurotypicals don't have].*

Work

- *Hi [NAME], I was hoping to share something about myself with you so you can understand a little bit more about me and how I work. I have Sensory Processing Disorder (SPD), a neurological difference that impacts how my brain makes sense of [ADD YOUR CHALLENGING SENSES HERE]. I wanted you to know because it means you might see me [TURN OFF EXTRA LIGHTS, USE A WEIGHTED LAP PAD, WEAR TINTED GLASSES, WEAR HEADPHONES, NEEDING A QUIET BREAK SOMETIMES—PICK SOMETHING TO PUT HERE]. But don't worry, I love my job and am so happy to be on your team. I'm glad to answer questions about it and send you some information [SEND THEM TO MY WEBSITE OR TO THE STAR INSTITUTE].*

Want to create your own from scratch? Hell yes! Think of it like an addition problem (yet another opportunity for you to join me in some Sky Math, woooot):

> Here's what's going on with me + Here's what it means + Here's why it matters + Here's what I need from you =
>
> Advocating for yourself like a champ

(P.S. Don't forget to throw in some nice things, like "thanks for caring about me" or "I'm grateful for your help"—kindness will always make people want to take your side.)

Maybe spend a few minutes making a list of the things you want people to know when they ask you questions about your sensory challenges. Pretend for a second that you're them and want to learn more about what it means to have SPD. What would you want to know? How would you want things explained? And then use those ideas to help you build your speech.

It almost doesn't matter which words you choose. Just be honest, and just be you. People's reactions to who you are will tell you a lot about them, the situation you're in, and how to shift your life accordingly.

Mostly, I encourage you to be brave. Sensory differences shift during our lifetimes, but you're always going to live with them in one way or another, so why not learn to talk about them now? The sooner you learn to put your arms around who you are, the happier you'll be as you finish growing up.

CHAPTER 11

Treatment, Tools, and Techniques

What makes SPD survivable? The treatments, tools, and techniques that exist out there for you to manage your sensitivities. If you were diagnosed with SPD when you were younger, you might already be doing some of these things. If you're just figuring out that you have SPD, some of these might be new to you. Or, like me, you'll realize you've been creating your own tools to meet the needs you've had since you were little. Not all of them will work, but some might make the world feel a little more you-friendly.

Let's start with the biggest thing.

Occupational Therapy (OT)

SPD and OT go together like two popular things you love that no one over 20 knows about. I can't even pretend I know what these things are, but you know what I mean. Usually where one goes, the other follows.

Occupational therapists think of living as a job, and they support people to make it easier for them to live in their environment. For people with SPD, occupational therapists help teach the brain how to respond better to sensory input. They basically do this by forcing you to have fun. There are swings and ball pits, sand and weights. It's a gym meets the things you loved most about being a kid in one place. And while you're having fun and feeling like a human burrito, your brain is doing magical things that will help you feel better in the world.

Psychotherapy

Therapy. You're probably not so excited about this one (or, maybe like me, you're secretly in love with the way the mind works). I get the sense most teens aren't trying to sneak into therapy sessions, but therapy is really important. It's a place where you can let all of the garbage out: how you feel about your parents, your siblings, your school life, your romantic life. You can yell and scream, cry and withdraw. You can share your deepest secrets.

Think of it like this: your therapist's job is to help you hold any heavy bags you're carrying, so you don't have to carry them alone. If having SPD makes you feel a certain way, you can say it out loud. For me, there's something about saying stuff out loud that makes it feel less intense. Swirling around in my brain, thoughts sound different, but saying them out loud makes them very real or not at all. I've said things to my therapist and have been like, *hahaha, no, that's clearly ridiculous now that I'm sharing it.* Therapy makes you feel good because it puts some thoughts in order. It quiets other thoughts down so you can put them to bed. It helps you wrap your arms around who you are, sensory differences and all.

* * * * * * * * * * * *

There are other therapies, but IMHO, the two I just mentioned are probably the best place for you to start. You can also talk to your family about physical therapy; some physical therapists work with sensory people to help strengthen the vestibular system. You can also find optometrists who do vision therapy to help strengthen your visual processing. But I encourage you to start somewhere if you haven't yet. Yes, you'll always live with your sensory differences, but there are ways to make things a little easier on you as you get older.

Speaking of ways to make things easier ...

Tools

If you did nothing for your sensory differences but add a few tools to your life, you'd be making a huge difference. Tools for SPD are very specific, but I've also learned they can be pretty much anything that helps take the pressure off of an uncomfortable sense or add in extra from a sense you like.

First: the formal tools.

Wilbarger Deep Pressure Brush

Imagine an oval bar of creamy white soap and add bristles to the bottom; this is exactly what a Wilbarger Deep Pressure Brush looks like. It's like something your mom uses to clean dishes, except it's weirdly soft and might feel good on your skin. (I'm obsessed with mine.) The theory behind it is it helps your brain and body calm down through deep stimulation of your skin. No one's researched it. Lots of professional people aren't sure about it. I think it's brilliant and would be happy to star in a one-woman study about why the little disc of plastic feels SO. STUPID. GOOD.

If you see an OT, they might have you use one a few times a day. Take it from me: bathroom stalls are good places to brush your skin like you're a show pony. Use your brush in a more public space, and be ready to talk about your sensory differences, because people are clearly going to be curious.

Fidgets

I crave touch, so I usually say my fingertips are hungry. As a kid, I would run my hands across my grandma's furry coats, especially when she just came in from the cold; cold and soft make my hands happy. I clung to my best pal, my stuffed lion named Leo (disclosure: still possibly my best friend decades later), because he was soft and his nose was covered with stone and velvet. I asked for little furry collectible animal figurines— not because I'm some great animal lover, but because they fit in the palm of my hand and I could rub them.

These are fidgets. They're little items that are meant to be fidgeted with, touched, stroked, twisted, smushed, and tossed between your fingers. They're usually smooth or bumpy, heavy, even sometimes squishy. Stress balls and slime are fidgets. Fidget spinners and cubes are … well, clearly fidgets because *fidget* is in their name. Anything you play with that makes you feel relaxed and keeps your fingertips happy is a fidget. Fidgeting helps me focus and calm down when I'm feeling scattered and overwhelmed by sensory input, emotions, or life in general.

Thinking about getting a fidget? Congratulations, your life is about to become awesome. You might want to consider something smooth and cold like hematite stones, a koosh or stress ball, putty, or even something fake-fur-trimmed. There are no rules. You just might need to be extra creative when you're at school or out with friends. It's hard to pass off a toy as a thing you need to carry around as a teen. Sometimes, pens and pen caps make all the difference. I've also used holding boyfriends' hands as fidgets before. Looks like I'm just being romantic, but there's a little something extra in it for me.

Earplugs

I need earplugs. I love earplugs. Earplugs are the reason I sleep well at night (outside of my delicious weighted blanket—keep reading for more on that). They're easy to carry around, you can pop them in your ears without anyone noticing, and most neurotypical people have used them, so you don't have to have a long discussion about them with anyone.

My favorite kind is made of foam by Hearoes. I like the 33db plugs when I'm sleeping, and 32db when I'm awake and need to function but also need some quiet. I once tried a generic store brand, and they left my ear canal all sorts of colorful, so I tossed them. Unless you're excited about becoming the next modern art project, pick something else.

Earmuffs

No, they're not the keep-your-ears-warm-in-winter kind (although, I mean, I guess you could use them like that if you can't find your fluffy ones). These earmuffs are like earplugs that cover your ears from the outside. Or maybe like those cool vintage headphones that make you look like you really *get* music. Their job is to cut down the amount of sound you have to process. Either way, if sticking earplugs in your ears make you feel like saying "Yuck," you might like these.

Noise-Canceling Headphones

Okay, so I don't actually own these. They're expensive—but from what I've been told, they're worth it if you're super-duper sensitive to sound. Instead of lowering sound, they're said to cancel sound entirely. Apparently, there's a microphone in the headphones that picks up on background noise and makes it go away, like some sort of sorcery. Some actually cancel sound, while others block sound.

But, like, yes please.

Tinted Glasses

My first pair of tinted glasses were sunglasses I snagged at a street fair. They were dark-blue tinted aviators that made me look like I'd stepped out of the 1970s, and I loved them immediately. They let me see the world around me smoothly, with less sharp edges. It was like my brain was able to take a deep breath for the first time ever. I noticed that I was better able to process the whole of a thing or person and not just the details with the glasses on my face.

But at work and in grad school, I felt like I looked insane. Strangers, classmates, and coworkers turned their heads as I passed by—because really, who wears sunglasses indoors—especially such big, old-timey ones? I was known as The Girl with the Blue Sunglasses (yet another title I considered for this book). People asked me about them all the time. I should've just worn a big button that said, "Ask Me About My SPD."

And then I went to see an eye doctor who worked with people with sensory issues, and I learned something cool. There was actual *science* behind my love of my blue glasses. YAAAS.

Let's see if I can break it down for you:

Colorful lenses stop some types of light from reaching your eyes. Blue lenses are especially liked by people with SPD because it calms down the brain and cuts down on the flickering of fluorescent lights (which most people don't notice at all). There are two pathways in your brain that help you see, and both need to be balanced for a happy visual experience. But for people with sensory differences, one pathway is overstimulated and the other isn't. So, looking through a blue tint activates one pathway and balances them both out. Our brains have trouble doing it for us, so the glasses do it instead. Brilliant.

If your eyes feel like they can't make sense of the visual world, see if you can wear a pair of colorful, tinted glasses to help.

Weighted Blanket

It's very simple: I'm in love with weighted blankets. For nighttime or naptime, they are magical tools that help my body feel safe and connected to the world around me so I can sleep. I'd seriously walk around with one draped across me if it were socially acceptable. Please, can we start a weighted blanket fashion movement?

I am a lucky lady: I own three weighted blankets and am borrowing a fourth. I have two main kinds that I think you should consider if you're looking for a blanket. One is a more traditional, cozy blanket with pellets that sound like gentle rain when you shift around (Magic Blanket), and the other is a beautiful (and silent) woven blanket with spaces between the weave to keep you cool (Bearaby—Cotton Napper). I love them both and use them for different purposes (I clearly nap and lounge with the Napper), and they're so different that I'd encourage you to check them both out. But seriously, it's hard to go wrong with a weighted blanket if you have proprioceptive challenges and need help falling asleep.

However, if you get a weighted blanket, be sure to pick one that's 10% of your body weight + 1lb (more Sky Math, hooray!) It's the right therapeutic weight for your body. I have one that's a few pounds heavier than I need, and while I don't mind it, it doesn't feel as balanced as the one that's the exact right weight.

Best Weighted Blanket Formula:

10% of your body weight + 1 pound

Weighted Sleep Mask

Weighted sleep masks are like a weighted blanket for your face. (I can hear the commercial now. Let me go copyright that …) I have two and am totally obsessed with them, especially when they're paired with a weighted blanket. If you have visual sensitivities, they block the light, and just like the weighted blanket, they help your body know where it is in space when you go to sleep.

Weighted Lap Pad

Because I clearly don't have enough weights in my life, I've also added two weighted lap pads to my Weighted Stuff collection. They're like mini weighted blankets for your lap (perfect for daytime hours and activities, as well as travel), and can help you focus in school, whether you're in person or at a distance. Once again, people with proprioceptive issues, especially those whose systems ignore input from this sense, will feel calmer and more connected sitting under a weighted lap pad.

Trampoline

Even as a little kid, I loved to jump. Watch any of my family's old home movies from when I was around four, and you'll see me bouncing across the screen with the widest smile on my face. Of course I was smiling—jumping engages the knee joints and helps with proprioception, which, as we all know, is a very powerful and regulating sense. Jumping was and still is one of my favorite things.

For a while, I had my own trampoline in my apartment. I loved taking friends around the space, because when they came upon a random trampoline, they'd always ask if I'd teleported in from a bizarre 1980s exercise video and where I was hiding my leg warmers. When I had my daughter, I thought infants and exercise equipment were a super bad idea and threw it out. Now that she's four, she has her own trampoline, and it's just small enough that I can't use it. But I love how much joy it brings her.

Dream of living in a sensory gym? Maybe ask for one. They're pretty cheap, and you can stand it up and lean it in a corner when you're done.

Chewables

Confession: I like biting things. Ice cubes, pretzels, fruit leather—and fingers, if they get in my way when I need to chew. Usually it happens when I've taken in too much sensory input and I'm overwhelmed. I'm always looking to chew and crunch with every meal and will actually not realize I've eaten if I don't shovel some crunchy foods in my mouth every few hours.

Input through your mouth can be very calming if you struggle with proprioception, and biting, chewing, and sucking are great for the jaw joints and the muscles around your mouth. Chewable jewelry exists, but it's not really easy to get away with gnawing on real things as a teen or adult, so maybe pick from some socially acceptable chewy things. No one, regardless of their wiring, will look at you funny if you pull out a stick of gum in a sensory moment.

Smellables

Overwhelmed by unfamiliar smells? Try sniffing something like essential oils, scented lotions, soaps, or hand sanitizers. Find a scent or two that are soothing to you and carry them around with you, and take a whiff when other smells become an issue. Crave smells? Stop and smell the roses.

Herbal Tea

Can a drink be a tool? Who knows, but herbal tea is one of those instant-relaxation tools for me. There's something about the weight of a mug in my hand and the repetitive motion of lifting the mug to my mouth that calms me down every time.

Usually I want things ice-cold, but I love pushing my face against the steam rising from a cup of tea and enjoying the heat. My favorites are lavender, chamomile, and Sleepytime—anything to calm me down, especially before bed, when my brain and senses are racing.

Techniques

So, these things aren't quite tools and they're not actually therapies; they're little activities and exercises I've learned to do when I need some extra support. You don't need to go anywhere or bring anything. All you need is yourself and maybe a little bit of guidance from me.

Humming

Humming a song is one of those things I do when I need to connect to my body and the world around me. Also, maybe you've noticed, but many people with SPD like to talk loudly. It's possible that hearing ourselves echo within our bodies is grounding. Scientists think humming might've once been a way for early humans to let their family know that they were okay and not in danger. It also engages a nerve that keeps the heart rate constant and controls digestion, so it's also a way for us to tell our bodies we're okay.

Deep Breathing

Breathe in slowly ... and breathe out again. Tell me that didn't feel good. Deep breathing is such a quick and easy way to slow down and reconnect. It also increases how much oxygen is in your brain and triggers things in your body to actually make you calmer.

Ready to try it? Let's go.

Sit comfortably or lie down somewhere that is sensory-friendly and close your eyes. Put your hands on your stomach. Breathe in through your nose while slowly counting to five, then breathe out through your lips for while slowly counting to five. The way I describe it to my daughter is "Breathe in like you're smelling something yummy and breathe out like you're blowing out birthday candles." Feel your belly rise and fall under your hands, and try not to raise your chest. Continue to do this for the next few minutes. If you're feeling relaxed, you can change the count to eight or even ten.

If you really want to make magic happen, combine this with the next exercise.

Visualization

This basically means imagining scenes in your mind. It's like actively creating a dream that relaxes you.

Find some sensory-friendly space. Sit or lie down in a comfortable position and close your eyes. You can start with a few deep breaths. Begin to imagine a safe place; it can be real or made up. Is it a cozy corner of your bedroom? Your best friend's backyard? Your favorite beach? The mosh pit of your favorite concert? A castle on a hill? Under the covers of your bed? Picture all of it: the sights, smells, sounds, feel. What color is the sky? How does your cat feel in your arms? Whatever is part of this scene, put yourself there in as much detail as you can imagine. Keep deep breathing. Don't you feel calmer?

Hitting the Deck

Okay, so I made this one up. I've found that before and during a sensory meltdown and during and after a sensory shutdown, I need to connect my whole body to something to feel safe again. I've tried lying on my bed, but it's not enough, so I sprawl out on my back on the floor, and I call it "hitting the deck." I swear it works. Why it works makes sense too: pressing your whole body against a surface is a great way to reconnect with your proprioceptive sense, which is calming and regulating. I go from overloaded, dark, and stormy to groggy, peaceful, and a little dopey 10-20 minutes later. It always feels like I'm waking up from a dream, and I always feel better. For extra calm points, add a weighted blanket—and cry if you need that release, too.

CHAPTER 12
Forward into the future

Check you out, Rockstar, you finished the book! WOOO. (Or you skipped ahead and missed some important things, in which case you fail and I'm going to have to mark it on your Permanent Record. Quick, go back and read stuff!) Assuming you got here by reading, I'm hoping you learned some new things about yourself. By now, you should be able to explain the science behind SPD, know what to say when you pull a teacher aside to disclose, and how to go about planning for a date. You should have a bunch of new tools to turn to when you're feeling overwhelmed. I hope you feel like you're a bit more of an expert now on what makes you *you*. And because this is a book, you can always turn back the pages and reread the chapters you need right when you need them. Books are cool like that.

Now that you have my little cheat-sheet for a sensory teen-agehood (the last title I considered for this book, I swear) what comes next is up to you. Are you going to speak up the next time your friends make plans? Will you think differently about college or your first job? Can you find a way to make peace with what you see on social media? (We're all still working on that one, FYI.) You're ultimately the star of your own future. You're in charge of how you live with your sensory differences.

This book was hard for me to write. Reliving teenagehood isn't always sunshine and bubblegum, and doing so reminded me how tough it is to be a teen. I'm sure sometimes it feels hard to be you, differently wired and all. But I also know that you're capable of doing so many things. How do I know this? Because I was capable too, even though it didn't always feel that way. In spite of the shutdown-causing marionette, even though I had unnamed episodes wherever I went, I had friends and boyfriends, a family that loved me, good grades, and a plan for a future. Here I am, sitting in that future. It's not exactly how I imagined it would be, but I made it here.

Mostly, you should know you're not alone. I hope my personal stories have proven that to you so many years later. It proved it to me as I wrote this book. The teenage me who you saw sitting on the stoop of that souvenir shop freaking out over a noisy French puppet? The teenage me alone in the bathroom of that clacking, clapping restaurant the following night? She didn't realize what was really going on.

I couldn't see then that a whole group of people just like me—including grown-up me—were really looking back through time at what I was going through with understanding and kindness. Just like (I hope) you are right now. We're never really alone, are we? We're always only a few memories away from ourselves. And in the sensory community, there's always someone else like us who gets it. I wasn't the first person to ever have a sensory shutdown, and I won't be the last one either.

Funny to think that somewhere out there in time is the future you, too. Maybe you're 38 years old just like me, sitting and looking back on the things you've done to get you to where you are. What do you think future you would want to see happen in your life in spite of—or even thanks to—your sensory differences? What can you do to make those things happen?

What do you think you'd scream back through time at teenage you reading this now?

Is it: *keep going?*

Is it: *give it a try?*

Is it: *you've got this?*

Is it: *wait 'til you see what*

Is it: *stay strong?*

happens next?

RACHEL

For me it's: *you're in good company.*
And always: *it's going to be okay.*

Listen closely. Be thoughtful. Be brave. Be you. Remember, you're building your bones, even as you read these words—so be kind, especially to yourself.

THE AUTHOR

Rachel S. Schneider, M.A., MHC is the award-winning author of *Sensory Like You* and *Making Sense: A Guide to Sensory Issues* and a delayed-diagnosis SPD adult. In the last decade, her advocacy efforts via Coming to My Senses have had a meaningful impact on the adult and teen SPD community. Rachel lives in New York City with her daughter.

ACKNOWLEDGEMENTS

When I pitched the idea for this book, I wasn't aware that my life was about to change in such surreal, significant, and painful ways. While none of the words say it directly, the writing of this book charts the strange path I've had to walk in the past year and a half. When I talk about being on one side of a cliff with a huge drop and landing at the other side, I'm referring to me—someone different from the person who wrote the first words you read. I share these personal details here because it means my thanks is much deeper than I could've ever fathomed.

Thank you to Rose Heredia-Bechtel and Jennifer Gilpin Yacio at Future Horizons for flexing with me as I faced unspeakable and unprecedented challenges. There were a few times I thought this book would never be finished, but your generosity with time gave me the space I needed to heal and create.

Endless love to Kelly Dillon, who stepped into the void left behind without question and generously became my illustrator and cover art guru for the third time. I'm so lucky to know you.

Gratitude to Sarah Norris for taking time to write such a personal and beautiful foreword. I'm thankful for your friendship.

To my friends—all of you—thank you for helping to pick me up and dust me off. Your strength made me strong, and it's one of the reasons I've made it to the end of this book and moved on to my next chapter.

To the man who brought sunshine back into my life, I am as I ever was and ever shall be ...

To my aunt, uncle, and cousins: I treasure your support and love in all areas of my life.

Love to my cousin Lauren. I credit you with my sanity through the chaos and don't know what I'd do without you.

To my sister and brother-in-law and my two delicious nieces, thank you for loving me as unconditionally as I love you.

Eternal thanks to my parents, who are my twin pillars of strength—my human scaffolding, my safety net in the flesh. If I stand and move through this world, it's because I know you're both walking near me.

A universe of love to my daughter, who saves me every single day purely by existing.

And finally, a lifetime of gratitude to the friends, boyfriends, teachers, and coworkers who helped shape my teenage years and brought this book to life. You will always and forever be a part of me.

DID YOU LIKE THE BOOK?

Rate it and share your opinion.

amazon.com   **BARNES & NOBLE**
BOOKSELLERS
www.bn.com

Not what you expected? Tell us!

Most negative reviews occur when the book did not reach expectation. Did the description build any expectations that were not met? Let us know how we can do better.

Please drop us a line at *info@fhautism.com*.
Thank you so much for your support!

CPSIA information can be obtained
at www.ICGtesting.com
Printed in the USA
JSHW051910190521
14891JS00002B/2